Holistic Happiness

Holistic Happiness

Spirituality and a Healing Lifestyle

Robert P. Vande Kappelle

WIPF & STOCK · Eugene, Oregon

HOLISTIC HAPPINESS
Spirituality and a Healing Lifestyle

Copyright © 2022 Robert P. Vande Kappelle. All rights reserved. Except for brief quotations in critical publications or reviews, no part of this book may be reproduced in any manner without prior written permission from the publisher. Write: Permissions, Wipf and Stock Publishers, 199 W. 8th Ave., Suite 3, Eugene, OR 97401.

Wipf & Stock
An Imprint of Wipf and Stock Publishers
199 W. 8th Ave., Suite 3
Eugene, OR 97401

www.wipfandstock.com

PAPERBACK ISBN: 978-1-6667-4776-8
HARDCOVER ISBN: 978-1-6667-4777-5
EBOOK ISBN: 978-1-6667-4778-2

06/20/22

Unless otherwise noted, Bible quotations are from the *New Revised Standard Version of the Bible*, copyright © 1989 by the Division of Christian Education of the National Council of the Churches of Christ in the United States of America. Used by permission.

To go deep in any one place is to meet
the infinite aliveness that is God,
for God is everywhere!

Contents

Preface | ix

1. Spiritual and Developmental Models of Life | 1
2. Holistic Pain | 22
3. Holistic Healing | 39
4. Holistic Theology | 54
5. Holistic Happiness | 72
6. Holistic Loving | 89
7. Holistic Work | 108
8. Holistic Consuming | 124
9. Holistic Eating and Exercise | 140
10. Holistic Creativity | 155

Bibliography | 171
Index | 175

Preface

GOOD HEALTH IS ONE of life's greatest blessings. It requires good genes, a balanced lifestyle, supportive companions, wholesome eating and drinking, regular exercise, a positive mindset, an active disposition, and good fortune. While good health is frequently disrupted by accidents, disease, stress, chemical and emotional imbalance, and numerous other factors, wellness is achievable and sustainable, but it requires balanced input from an individual's four constituent dimensions: physical, mental, emotional, and spiritual.

While bodily health is the most discernible form of personal wellbeing, overall wellness derives from a person's innermost spirit, which then animates and energizes the soul or emotional center, the mind or cognitive center, and through them the body and its physical organs.[1] As the healing sciences now acknowledge, physical healing, necessary when homeostasis is internally or externally disrupted, involves attending to biological, psychological, social, and spiritual dimensions of illness.

The biopsychosocial model, a modern holistic view of human beings now increasingly used in health sciences, was introduced to medicine by George L. Engel (1913–1999), a prominent scholar engaged in the psychosomatic movement. He claimed that in order to better understand and respond to patients' needs, physicians should simultaneously attend to the biological, psychological, and social dimensions of an illness. This approach views suffering, disease, and illness as affected by multiple factors, from societal to molecular. At a practical level, it is a way of understanding

---

1. A fourfold understanding of anthropology is supported biblically (see Mark 12:30) and religiously (see Smith, *Forgotten Truth*, 63–95).

the patient's subjective experience as an essential contributor not only to human care and accurate diagnosis, but also to health outcome.[2]

In recent decades, humanization of medicine and empowerment of patients have been improved by including the patient's subjective experience, by expanding the causational framework of disease, by valuating the patient-clinician relationship, and by giving expanding roles to the patient in clinical decision-making. In 1948, the World Health Organization (WHO) adopted the following definition of health: "Health is a state of complete physical, mental, and social well-being, and not merely the absence of disease or infirmity." This definition, while expansive, lacked reference to the spiritual dimension of life. However, in 1999, the 52nd Assembly of this institution proposed some amendments to its constitution. One of the proposed modifications was the insertion of spiritual well-being into its concept of health. The new text became, "Health is a dynamic state of complete physical, mental, spiritual, and social well-being and not merely the absence of disease or infirmity." Despite approval, the new version was eventually rejected, partly because of the ambiguous nature and the multiple meanings of the concept of spirituality, though the WHO continues to highlight the importance of the spiritual dimension for clinical purposes.

Currently, many researchers are expanding the biopsychosocial model to include the spiritual dimension. One such researcher is David A. Katerndahl, whose study "Impact of Spiritual Symptoms and Their Interactions on Health Services and Life Satisfaction" demonstrates the relevance of spirituality for understanding health outcomes.[3] Likewise, Daniel P. Sulmasy justifies the expansion of the model to psychosocial-spiritual by noting that genuinely holistic health care must address the totality of the patient's relational existence. According to Sulmasy, this expansion will contribute to a model of care and research that takes account of patients in their entirety.[4] Psychologists are now referring to this integrative model of addiction and recovery as the Bio-Psycho-Social-Spiritual Model (BPSS). This approach maintains that healing, like illness, represents a complex interaction between biological, psychological, social, and spiritual forces.

---

2. Saad, "A True Biopsychosocial-Spiritual Model?"
3. Katerndahl, "Impact of Spiritual Symptoms," 412–20.
4. Sulmasy, "Biopsychosocial-Spiritual Model," 24–33.

Preface

Note for Leaders and Participants

Holistic Happiness is useful for individual or group study. As you read this book, consider journaling as a way to grow spiritually. A good place to start is with your hopes and dreams. As you reflect and write, be honest with your thoughts and feelings, without ignoring your fears. Transparency facilitates the process of becoming healthy and whole.

Each chapter concludes with questions for discussion or reflection. Write the answers to each question in your journal, in addition to the questions below, which are appropriate for each chapter. If you are reading this book in a group setting, be prepared to share your answers with others in the group. If your study is private, I encourage you to write answers to each question in your journal for review and further reflection. Leaders may select questions from these lists that they deem most helpful to group discussion. Upon completing each chapter, readers will find the following general questions helpful as well.

1. After reading this chapter, what did you learn about spirituality?
2. In your estimation, what is the primary insight gained from this chapter?
3. *For personal reflection*: Does this chapter raise any issues you need to handle or come to terms with successfully? If so, how will you deal with them?

1

Spiritual and Developmental Models of Life

MOST HUMANS, ANCIENT AND modern alike, pattern their lives after some model, whether consciously or unconsciously. These models can be biological, social, psychological, cognitive, moral, ecological, religious, existential, or mystical. Healthy individuals are said to go through discernible stages of growth throughout their lifetime.[1]

According to psychologist Erik Erikson (1902–1994), psychosocial development proceeds by critical steps, described as infancy (birth to 18 months), early childhood (2 to 3 years of age), preschool (3 to 5 years), school age (6 to 11 years), adolescence (12 to 18 years), young adulthood (19 to 40 years), middle adulthood (40 to 65 years), and maturity (65 to death). Each stage is marked by crisis, connoting not a catastrophe but a turning point, a crucial period of increased vulnerability and heightened potential. At such points achievements are won or failures occur, leaving the future to some degree better or worse but in any case, restructured. For each stage Erikson defined a basic conflict, important events, and outcomes.

The strength acquired at one stage is tested by the necessity to transcend it, meaning that the individual is able to take chances in the next stage with what was most vulnerably precious in the previous one. For example, healthy children will not fear life if their elders have integrity enough not to fear death.

A second developmental model is that of Lawrence Kohlberg (1927–1987), an American psychologist best known for his theory of stages of

---

1. The material on Erikson, Kohlberg, and Fowler is adapted from Vande Kappelle, *Dark Splendor*, 7–15.

moral development. He delineates six stages of development, from pre-conventional to post-conventional morality as follows:

Pre-Conventional Morality

Stage 1: Obedience or Punishment Orientation
This is the stage that all young children start at (and a few adults remain in). Rules are seen as being fixed and absolute. Obeying the rules is important because it means avoiding punishment

Stage 2: Self-Interest Orientation
As children grow older, they begin to see that other people have their own goal and preferences and that often there is room for negotiation. Decisions are made based on the principle of "What's in it for me?" For example, an older child might reason: "If I do what mom or dad wants me to do, they will reward me. Therefore I will do it."

Conventional Morality

Stage 3: Social Conformity Orientation
By adolescence, most individuals have developed to this stage. There is a sense of what "good boys" and "nice girls" do and the emphasis is on living up to social expectations and norms because of how they impact day-to-day relationships.

Stage 4: Law and Order Orientation
By the time individuals reach adulthood, they usually consider society as a whole when making judgments. The focus is on maintaining law and order by following the rules, doing one's duty and respecting authority.

Post-Conventional Morality

Stage 5: Social Contract Orientation
At this stage, people understand that there are differing opinions out there on what is right and wrong and that laws are really just a social contract based on majority decision and inevitable compromise. People at this stage sometimes disobey rules if they find them to be inconsistent with their personal values and will also argue for certain laws to be changed if they are no longer "working." Our modern democracies are based on the reasoning of Stage 5.

Stage 6: Universal Ethics Orientation
Few people operate at this stage all the time. It is based on abstract reasoning and the ability to put oneself in other people's shoes. At this stage,

people have a principled conscience and will follow universal ethical principles regardless of what the official laws and rules are.

As humans grow by progressing physically, psychologically, emotionally, and even intellectually, so they undergo various stages of growth in their faith. Out of one's individuality flows a spirituality that also yearns for growth and expression. What Erikson contributed to our understanding of the stages of psychosocial development and Lawrence Kohlberg to the stages of moral development, so James Fowler (1940–2015) did for spirituality in developing seven stages of faith, from stage zero, called "primal faith," when infants and toddlers develop (or fail to develop) a sense of safety about the universe and the divine, to a sixth stage called "universalizing faith," a rarely reached stage of those who live their lives to the full in service of others without any real fears or worries. Most people plateau at what Fowler calls the "synthetic-conventional" stage, one arising in adolescence. At this stage authority is usually placed in individuals or groups that represent one's beliefs.

Fowler's stages of faith are described as

Stage 0: Primal Faith (0 to 2 years): This stage is characterized by early learning the safety of the environment. Under consistent nurture, children develop a sense of safety about the universe and the divine. Negative experiences (neglect and abuse) lead to distrust of the universe and the divine.

Stage 1: Intuitive-Projective (3 to 7 years): This is the stage of preschool children in which fantasy and reality often are mixed together. However, during this stage, our most basic ideas about God are usually learned from our parents and/or society.

Stage 2: Mythic-Literal (mostly in school children): When children become school-age, they start understanding the world in more logical ways. They generally accept the stories told to them by their faith community but tend to understand them in very literal ways. [Some people remain in this stage through adulthood.]

Stage 3: Synthetic-Conventional (arising in adolescence; ages 12 to adulthood): Most people move on to this stage as teenagers. At this point, their lives have grown to include several different social circles, which they need to pull together. When this happens, a person usually adopts some sort of all-encompassing belief system. However, at this stage, people tend to have a hard time seeing outside their box, not recognizing that they are "inside" a belief system. At this stage, authority is usually placed in individuals or groups that represent one's beliefs. [A great many adults remain in this stage.]

Stage 4: Individuative-Reflective (usually mid-twenties to late thirties): This is the tough stage, often begun in young adulthood, when people start seeing outside the box and realizing that there are other "boxes." They begin to examine their beliefs critically on their own and often become disillusioned with their former faith. Ironically, the Stage 3 people usually think that Stage 4 people have become "backsliders" when in reality they have actually moved forward.

Stage 5: Conjunctive Faith (mid-life crisis): It is rare for people to reach this stage before mid-life. This is the point when people begin to realize the limits of logic and start to accept life's paradoxes. As they begin to see life as a mystery, they often return to sacred stories and symbols but this time without remaining in a theological box.

Stage 6: Universalizing Faith (enlightened stage): Few people reach this stage; those who do, live their lives to the full in service of others without real worry or spiritual doubt.

In his book, *A Different Drum*, M. Scott Peck provides the following simplified version of Fowler's stages:

1. *Chaotic-Antisocial*—People in this stage are usually self-centered and often find themselves in trouble due to unprincipled living. If they do finally embrace the next stage, it often occurs in a very dramatic way.

2. *Formal-Institutional*—At this stage people rely on some sort of institution (such as a church) to give them stability. They become attached to the forms of their religion and become extremely upset when these are called into question.

3. *Skeptic-Individual*—Those who break with the previous stage usually do so when they start seriously questioning previously held values and beliefs. Frequently they end up non-religious and some stay here permanently.

4. *Mystical-Communal*—People who reach this stage start to realize that there is truth to be found in the previous two stages and that life can be paradoxical and mysterious. Those who reach this stage emphasize communal rather than individual concerns.

Spiritual and Developmental Models of Life

First and Second Half of Life

Of the many models regarding spirituality, one I find compelling is known as the "second half of life." This "further journey" is not chronological, nor does one magically stumble upon it at midlife or in times of crisis, though these often serve as catalysts. While the second journey represents the culmination of one's faith journey, it is largely unknown today, even by people we consider deeply religious, since most individuals and institutions remain stymied in the preoccupations of the first half of life, establishing identity, creating boundary markers, and seeking security. The first-half-of-life task, while essential, is not the full journey. Furthermore, one cannot walk the second journey with first-journey tools. One needs a new toolkit.

The first task is to build a strong "container" or identity; the second is to find the contents that the container is meant to hold.[2] The first task—surviving successfully—is obvious, one we take for granted as the purpose of life. We all want to complete successfully the task that life first hands us: establishing an identity, a home, a career, relationships, friends, community, and security, all foundational for getting started in life. Many cultures throughout history, most empires in antiquity, and the majority of individuals in the modern period have focused on first-half-of-life tasks, primarily because it is all they have time for, but also for lack of vision.

Most of us are never told that we can set out from the known and the familiar to take on a further journey. Our institutions, including our churches, are almost entirely configured to encourage, support, reward, and validate the tasks of the first half of life. Shocking and disappointing as it may be, we struggle more to survive than to thrive, focusing on "getting through" or on getting ahead rather than on finding out what is at the top or was already at the bottom. As wilderness guide Bill Plotkin puts it, many of us learn to do our "survival dance," but we never get to our actual "sacred dance."

According to Plotkin, the stage of adolescence—beyond which most adults never move—holds the key to both individual development and human evolution. In this stage individuals develop their distinctive ego-based consciousness, which represents both their greatest liability as well as their greatest potential. If they are to become fully human and move to the stages of genuine adulthood, people in the adolescent stage must let go of the familiar and comfortable while submitting to a journey of descent into "the mysteries of nature and the human soul." Individuals who remain within

---

2. Rohr, *Falling Upward*, xiii.

the constraints of a largely adolescent world regress into "pathological adolescence," characterized by materialism, sexism, competitive violence, racism, egoism, and self-destructive patterns. Patho-adolescent societies are perpetuated by leaders and celebrities described as self-serving politicians, moralizing religious leaders, drug-induced entertainment icons, and greedy captains of industry. If society is going to develop soulcentrically, it must be overseen by wise elders, not by adolescent politicians and corporate officers.

How can you know you are entering the second half of life? The following road markers are quite reliable: when you

- experience new urges
- sense a new vision
- are ready to let go of old securities
- are ready to risk giving up the patterns of the past for the promise of the future
- are ready to embrace your shadow self[3]
- are as focused on the "inner" life as on the outer dimension of life.

When speaking of life's journey, or more specifically, of a person's faith journey (including its religious and spiritual phases), it is beneficial to be guided by models, for all such journeys take place in particular contexts. All branches of religion/spiritual traditions around the world provide models for growth and progress within their tradition, including psychological, moral, and theological guidelines for sustained momentum.

Ancient Hindu society, for example, established a fourfold pattern for life, two stages for the social journey (student and householder phases), and two associated with the spiritual journey (retirement and homeless phases). The student phase begins after the rite of initiation, between the ages of eight and twelve, and lasts for twelve years. In this formative stage, proper behavior is cultivated and character is formed. The householder phase, viewed as the cornerstone of society, focuses on family, vocation,

---

3. The shadow self, something everyone possesses, represents the least developed part of one's personality. The shadow uses relatively childish and primitive forms of judgment and perception, often as an escape from the conscious personality and in defiance of conscious standards. One's shadow includes "good" qualities as well as "bad" or "shameful" qualities that one denies. As one makes room for one's polarities, one becomes healthier and more open to transforming grace.

and community. During the retirement phase, individuals can withdraw from social obligation to discover the meaning of life and prepare for their rebirth after death. The *sannyasin* stage, open to members of the upper classes at any time, consists of an ascetic and homeless lifestyle, designed to eliminate individuality in hope of experiencing unity with eternal reality, thereby ending the recurring pattern of transmigration.

As a corollary to this developmental model, Hindus also devised four spiritual paths, *yogas*, or means of salvation:

- *karma yoga* (a spirituality of works intended for persons of active bent)
- *bhakti yoga* (a spirituality of devotion intended for persons of emotional bend)
- *jnana yoga* (a spirituality of knowledge intended for persons of reflective bent), and
- *raja yoga* (a spirituality of liberation or self-actualization for persons who are scientifically or experimentally inclined).

Unlike Hindu spirituality, which developed four parallel spiritualities or paths of salvation, it is important to note the holistic approach Jesus used in addressing questions about how best to fulfill God's will. Viewing love as the fulfillment of the Great Commandment, Jesus emphasized that his followers love God and neighbor not conditionally or out of obligation but passionately and wholeheartedly, with all their heart, soul, mind, and strength (Mark 12:30), uniting the four Hindu paths of salvation into one commitment.

In the Christian tradition, the noted Danish philosopher Søren Kierkegaard (1813–1855), made an important contribution to the life of faith in his formulation of three levels of existence or stages through which humans go in their ascent toward God. On the first level, which he labeled the *aesthetic stage*, individuals are ruled by their senses, in which case they can be called "sensual aesthetes." Such persons live solely for the present, and particularly for self-gratification. Aesthetes, characterized by the absence of either moral standards or religious faith, remain detached and uncommitted. Kierkegaard extended this attitude to include "the intellectual aesthete," the contemplative person who tries to stand outside of life and behold it as a spectator.

The aesthetic life, however, is not ultimately fulfilling, for it ends in boredom and despair. Aesthetes, recognizing that they are living inauthentically, find no remedy on this level. They must either remain there in boredom and despair or make a transition to the next level by an act of choice. Willing, not thinking, is the key. The act of choosing does not resolve the tension, for one must *either* remain at the first level *or* choose to move on. The antithesis remains.

The second level, called *the ethical stage*, requires that one abandon attitudes of selfishness and make commitments to others. Here moral standards and obligations are adopted, as dictated by reason. Cold detachment is left behind, for in this stage one embraces universal standards. The example Kierkegaard chose as the transition from aesthetic to moral consciousness is marriage, in which a person renounces the satisfaction of the sexual impulse according to passing attraction and enters the state of marriage, accepting all its obligations. This stage is meaningful and superior to the aesthetic level because it provides continuity and stability to life.

Whereas Kierkegaard believed sincerely in universal moral obligations, this stage is not the end or goal of existence. The problem with the ethical stage is that the ethical person remains committed to autonomy and self-sufficiency. The ethical hero recognizes self-sufficiency as sin, but believes he can overcome it by sheer willpower and ability. Eventually the ethical person comes to the awareness of inability to fulfill the moral law and becomes conscious of guilt and estrangement from God. The ethical person is once more confronted with a choice: either to continue in one's effort to fulfill the moral law, or move to a higher stage, to a life of faith. This requires an act of commitment, which Kierkegaard called a "leap of faith." In his own life Kierkegaard had found that the previous stages were based upon the "illusion of humanism," resulting in failure to recognize need for God. The third and final stage, which he called *the religious stage*, entails a life of faith. This is final because it recognizes the existence of God and the need to relate oneself wholly to God.

In each previous stage, Kierkegaard selected a figure from literature or history as an example. For the aesthetic stage he chose Don Juan, the classic figure from Spanish drama who lived solely for sensual pleasure and was unable to commit to a meaningful relationship with others. The ethical stage is typified by Socrates, who took his own life rather than compromise his moral standards. The example he selected for the religious stage was Abraham, whose trust of God and unwavering obedience led him to choose to sacrifice his only son Isaac, even in the face of absurdity, for to question God would be to place reason over faith.

Is such behavior justifiable or is it unethical? In selecting this example, Kierkegaard was not denying the validity of ethics. He stated that the individual who is called to break with the ethical must first be ethical, that is, must first have subordinated to universal morality. The break, when one is called to make it, is made in "fear and trembling" and not arrogantly or proudly. In this final stage, the ethical is not abolished but dethroned by a higher purpose or end, a phenomenon he described as the "teleological suspension of the ethical." The key to this final stage is not the commendable humanistic goal of universal duty to others, but the unqualified giving of oneself to God. If one doesn't go beyond the ethical, beyond moral obligation, one cannot properly say that one is related to God, or obedient to God. Ethical duty, he believed, must ultimately lead to God, but since it usually leads to humanity (i.e. to humanism), then this stage must be transcended. An absolute relationship to an absolute (God) requires a relative relationship to relative ends. For Kierkegaard, everything other than God is relative.

Five Halves of Life

Understanding the term "half" symbolically rather than literally, it is possible to speak of five such dimensions or mindsets that people may acquire through life, including a preparatory stage or "half" (phase 0) and then two essentially secular/religious halves, which I call first and second half living and thinking (phases 1A and 1B), themselves mirroring two spiritual phases called first and second half of life spirituality (phases 2A and 2B), configured as follows:

1. Preparatory Half (phase 0): preconventional morality (childhood and adolescence)
2. First Half Living and Thinking (phase 1A): conventional morality (late adolescence through adulthood)
3. Second Half Living and Thinking (phase 1B): postconventional morality (late adolescence through adulthood)
4. First Half of Life Spirituality (phase 2A): conventional religiosity (late adolescence through adulthood)
5. Second Half of Life Spirituality (phase 2B): postconventional spirituality (late adolescence through adulthood).

Holistic Happiness

In this model, phase 0 corresponds to the Hindu pre-initiation stage, to Kohlberg's stages 1 and 2, to Fowler's stages 0, 1, and 2, as well as to Kierkegaard's sensual or aesthetic stage, in that at this stage of life, individuals are ruled by the senses, concerned primarily with self-gratification, and live for the present. Individuals in phase 0 (including most children, youth, adolescents, and some adults) may have special and unique spiritual dispositions and experiences, but such experience is immature and unformed. On the whole, their beliefs, behavior, and outlook is best characterized as preparatory or preconventional, since their character and personality, like their morality and brains, is mostly borrowed, imitated, untested, and not yet fully formed. This phase revolves around the mental function of sorting nearly everything into one of two categories (things are either permitted or prohibited, others are either friend or foe, and one is either happy or sad). For that reason, in stage 0, you set out to master the mental skills of dualism, of seeing the world in twos (this or that, in or out, right or wrong). Stage 0 is the baseline of what being raised means in our culture. Here one is taught the difference between right and wrong and other basic dualisms.

At some point in their socializing growth, youth begin accommodating to those around them, joining peer groups and aspiring to be admired and respected by others. Entering the first half of living and thinking, such individuals are shaping, developing, and testing their identity. Authorities—parents, grandparents, teachers, political and religious leaders—are central to this phase. Phase 1A is the phase of authority as well as of dualism. This phase corresponds to the Hindu student stage, to Kohlberg's stages 3 and 4, to Fowler's stage 5, and to initial aspects of Kierkegaard's ethical stage. While some individuals at this point become relatively autonomous, the majority desire to be like their elders, valuing and depending on their authority. They trust authorities and wish to please them, and they aspire to be as certain and all-knowing as they are. As far as they are concerned, the authorities know everything, and they do not, so they feel highly dependent on them. Before long, they find out that the authorities in their life dislike or distrust other authorities, and their dualism adds a new category: us versus them. This social dualism creates a strong sense of loyalty and identity among "us." It also creates a strong sense of anxiety and even hostility about "them," the "others," the "outsiders," and the "outcasts." Phase 1A is built on trust, because at that stage, trust is an absolute necessity, a matter of survival. Simple trust and unquestioning loyalty are what matters in phase 1A.

Spiritual and Developmental Models of Life

While this phase works well with adolescents and young adults, many people spend their entire lives in phase 1A, submitting to authorities and following all the rules. Then, when it is time for them to become authorities themselves, they demand the same submission from the next generation that they themselves gave to the previous generation. For that reason, it shouldn't be a surprise that faith and religion are a strictly phase 1A phenomenon for millions, even billions, of people.

Thus far, phase 1A may feel like a school to help people learn the basic morals necessary for independence. However, at some point, this phase becomes confining or restrictive, and individuals begin to question whether authorities are always right. They may even question whether rules are always absolute and appropriate. This may happen at twelve or twenty-two or forty-five, but eventually, many enter phase 1B. If phase 1A is about dualism and dependence, phase 1B is about pragmatism and independence. People in this phase recognize they have their own lives to live, and they have to find a way to become who they are on their own.

In phase 1A they were drawn to authority figures who told them what to think and do, but in phase 1B they seek out coaches who teach them how to think for themselves and help them develop their own goals, along with their own skills to attain those goals. In phase 1A they saw life as a matter of survival, but in phase 1B they see life as a game, as a contest of competing and winning. In phase 1A everything was either known or knowable, but in phase 1B, everything is learnable and doable, if only they can find the right models, mentors, and coaches, and master the right techniques, skills, and know-how. Phase 1B corresponds to the Hindu householder stage, to Kohlberg's stage 5, and to aspects of Kierkegaard's ethical and religious stages.

When people run into problems with phase 1A living and thinking, some may temporarily or permanently resort to stage 0 behavior and belief, living solely for pleasure and ego-gratification. However, many phase 1A individuals abandon dualism and pragmatism, together with authoritarian leaders, dogmatic mindsets, and moralistic standards, and commit instead to global and pluralistic values, loving others selflessly, simplifying lifestyle, living generously and compassionately, committing to social, ecological, political, and economic issues and concerns. Becoming atheists, agnostics, or merely nonbelievers, such individuals embody Fowler's stage 6, only achieving this stage secularly and nonspiritually.

While we are now familiar with the expression "the first and second halves of life," we should not, indeed we cannot equate them with first and second half of life spirituality. While there are similarities and overlap between these formulations, the first expression refers essentially to chronology, distinguishing immaturity from maturity, youth and adulthood from midage and old age, starting life from concluding life.

By contrast, first and second half of life spirituality, while often working in tandem with first and second half of life living and thinking, is a way of life and thought that though religious in nature, is centered on encounter with deity/divine Spirit, with opening to grace as the foundational event. However, for many if not for most individuals, piety, religion, morality, and even culture take the place of spirituality. In such cases, nominal religion becomes religiosity, a substitute for authentic spirituality, and in speaking of religiosity, we find we are no longer describing spirituality but rather an acculturated form of first half of life living and thinking. For many people, particularly those brought up in evangelical Christian homes, phase 1A (first half living and thinking) and phase 2A (first half of life spirituality) are experienced concurrently, for they find themselves living dualistically, adapting to secular and religious rules and guidelines simultaneously.

According to our model, it is quite natural for many children brought up in traditional Christian households to bypass phases 1A and 1B altogether and enter phase 2A spirituality at an early age. As is true of phase 1A, phase 2A, understood as a moral/religious phase common to evangelical Christianity, this stage is centered on acquiring essential religious beliefs and mastering dualistic mental skills such as sorting things into opposing categories such as right or wrong, true or false, sacred or secular, good and evil, and others as friends or foes. Authorities such as parents, teachers, and religious leaders are central to this way of being religious or spiritual. Similar to phase 1A, phase 2A commonly corresponds to the Hindu student phase, to Kohlberg's stages 3 and 4, and to Fowler's stage 3. However, unlike phase 1A, phase 2A incorporates elements of Kierkegaard's ethical and religious stages, in that it combines morality with a life of faith.

In my experience and from my vantage point as a scholar of spirituality and religious studies, the entry point to authentic spirituality, unlike much moral and religious belief and behavior, is not ritual or indoctrination, although these can be catalysts for first half of life spirituality, but rather a personal or individual encounter with the divine. This experience, called a "second birth" by evangelicals, profession of faith and baptism by Baptists, speaking in tongues or Spirit-filled living by Pentecostals, confirmation by Catholics, or Bar Mitzvah by Jews, is frequently the foundational

Spiritual and Developmental Models of Life

experience for first half of life spirituality. Such events are usually euphoric, but such euphoria is often short-lived, for this experience is frequently followed by conformity, rigid religious belief, and moralistic behavior.

Because phase 2A spirituality is highly dualistic, such dualism is divisive and, like phase 1A, it creates a strong sense of loyalty and identity. It also creates a strong sense of anxiety and even hostility toward "outsiders," "backsliders," and "outcasts." At some point in the faith journey, phase 2A believers are no longer content merely to listen to a sermon by an authority figure; they want to learn methods of studying the Bible for themselves. Learning and studying, thinking for themselves and reaching their own conclusions, are part of what it means to be a good phase 2A believer. Such people become active consumers in the religious market. Every year, they need more sermons, books, radio and TV shows, podcasts, conferences, courses, retreats, camps, churches, and mission trips. For some phase 2A people, their faith never exceeds the authoritarian, dualistic faith of phase 2A spirituality, while others never exceed the inquisitive, pragmatic side of dogmatic faith. Others, however, outgrow this phase altogether, questioning their religious goals, needs, and priorities.

When people run into problems with phase 2A spirituality, some transfer to another faith community. Other disillusioned phase 2A believers temporarily or permanently revert to phase 1 standards, perspectives, and forms of living. When phase 2A people find religious teaching or programming doesn't produce the results they expect, many sincere believers simply amp up their effort, assuming the fault is their own. Many modern individuals, however, experience a profound loss of religious confidence, and their phase 2A spirituality starts to collapse. For most such believers, there is no going back, at least not in the long term. Having felt increasingly alienated from phase 2A spiritual dualism and theological dogmatism, they lose faith in both authoritarian leaders and success coaches, whether inside or outside the church. Both types of leaders made promises they couldn't deliver, and neither type honestly faced life's deeper questions and challenges.

While some phase 2A believers start doubting the whole faith project, others aren't so easily satisfied. Their quest for honesty and depth burns like a fire in the belly and they move into phase 2B spirituality. If such phase 2A believers remain open and patient, many encounter a moment of crisis, and they find themselves actors in a deeper narrative that embraces and integrates all things, producing a way to see things whole again. This second awakening produces seekers, transformed by what might be called "an experience of sacred mystery." Something has happened to them—a mystical experience, something traumatic, a relationship, a sudden realization, a wilderness experience, an experience of "something more"—and the word "God" became meaningful once again, only this time not as a reference to a supernatural being "out there" but to the sacred at the center of existence, the holy mystery that is all around us and within us. No longer a mere idea or an article of belief external to oneself, God has become an element of experience. Such persons have reached phase 2B spirituality (also called *second naiveté*), a state where they participate in religious rituals because they are meaningful and not because they are required, where they hear ancient biblical stories as "true" while knowing them as not literally true.

Looking back, they discover that they still retain powerful and valuable treasures gained in previous phases. Though nondualists, they appreciate the lessons of dualism, which taught them to distinguish right from wrong and good from evil, and to care about their choices. From earlier phases, they also learned to be curious and flexible. They also learned that different phases of life operate by different sets of rules. In addition to becoming independent, self-motivated, and self-managed adults who take responsibility for their own successes and failures, they also learned that doubt and perplexity bring some of the greatest spiritual gifts life has to offer, gifts such as humility, honesty, courage, and sensitivity. Critical of their own critical thinking, skeptical of their own skepticism, they begin to wonder, hope, and imagine, and they dare to believe that there is a better second half of life, a better half of spirituality. To maintain momentum, to keep growing and developing, however, requires a kind of dying, a death to ego or pride, a relinquishment of our right to judge, to know, and to control. You might call this a death to privilege, superiority, or supremacy, as seekers realize that all people share in the human condition.

Phase 2B spirituality builds on "the still more excellent way of love" described by Paul in his letter to the Corinthians (1 Cor 12:31—14:1). In this passage, Paul makes clear that nearly everything religious people strive for will eventually be embraced by something deeper. Even faith and hope don't have the last word. Only love, he says, is the more excellent way. In this phase, we can finally accept that all our knowing, past and present, is partial (1 Cor 13:12). Phase 2B seekers finally see authority figures as mortal and fallible human beings. This awareness also allows them to find their identity in new ways in relation to others; not in phase 2A dependence on fallible authority figures but in the more mature interdependence of nonduality.

Spiritual and Developmental Models of Life

This humility before others morphs into the realization that no statement about God—or even about what is true—can be final or complete.

This new realization—likened to a second naiveté, a second simplicity or innocence best described as transcendence, combines the best of the conservative and the best of the progressive positions, because it brings along or includes the previous stages rather than leaving them behind. Phase 2B spirituality eventually matures into a higher spirituality, continuing in an ascending spiral of growth and discovery that lasts as long as life itself. Far from feeling they have finally arrived, phase 2B seekers finally begin to understand that arrival has never been the goal.

Corresponding to aspects of Hindu retirement and *sannyasin* stages as well as to Kohlberg's stage 6, Fowler's stage 6, and advanced existential aspects of Kierkegaard's religious stage, phase 2B spirituality allows seekers to discover amazing truths. For example, they discover that spirituality is about love; that knowing is loving; that they know ourselves by loving ourselves; that they know others by loving them; that they know God by loving ourselves and others. Those who reach phase 2B spirituality do not experience certainty, however, for that is the concern of those in earlier phases. Phase 2B seekers never feel they have arrived. They are not obsessed with misguided notions of certainty or supremacy—more the opposite. Committed to the faith journey, they know there is no such thing as certainty in faith. Faith, like all creativity, flourishes not in certainty but in questioning, not in security but in venturing. In phase 2B spirituality, it is trust that matters, and qualities such as peace, harmony, joy, relationships, intimacy, and unity.

While some form of awakening (spiritual conversion or "spiritual rebirth") may be foundational for second half of life spirituality, this experience differs from similar first half of life conversion in that for this second "half" of life, such an experience is not based on a decision one makes or a commitment one controls. Rather, this experience is an absolute gift of grace, for it comes more as a realization or revelation than as an act of the will. Unlike entrance into first half of life spirituality, this second experience is best described as a realization or awakening, for such transformation simply happens over time, more like a process than an event, and it may take time before individuals become conscious of the changes within themselves. More commonly, awareness occurs retrospectively, brought to our attention by those around us who notice the difference in our attitude, nature, and demeanor.

According to the five halves of life model, spirituality is not a specific way of living and thinking, nor a way of being moral or religious, but rather is a mature and selfless way of being. While first half of spirituality (phase 2A) may be initiated by individuals and can look like religious living and thinking, second half of spirituality (phase 2B) is initiated and led by the Divine Spirit. In both cases, individuals are oriented consciously and unconsciously toward the Divine, understood to be present both immanently and transcendently.

While individuals can describe their own experience of the second spiritual journey and even serve as mentors, they cannot define or outline the journey for others. This is due both to the uniqueness of the journey and to a subtle factor, known by generations of mystics and spiritual masters but elusive to many of our contemporaries: One does not choose this second spiritual journey; rather it chooses you. It finds you by means of your soul, your personal center and true home, the source of your true belonging. The soul comes to our aid through dreams, deep emotion, love, the quiet voice of guidance, synchronicities, revelations, hunches, and visions, and at times through illness, nightmares, and terrors. This is the identity that defines us, aligning us with our powers of nurturing, transforming, and creating, with our powers of presence and wonder. It is the soul that guides us, preparing the way and declaring us ready for this further journey.

As you may have guessed, the use of the phrase "five halves of life" in this chapter serves as a koan, that is, as an irrational riddle designed to stimulate your deepest intuition and to help you remain open to the limitless possibilities associated with spirituality. Viewed literalistically or on an elementary level, there can only be two halves of life, rather than three, four, or five. From this perspective, the five halves of life model is reducible to two halves or dimensions of life, one set of halves for the False Self or ego and one set for the True Self or soul, both preceded by a preparatory or preliminary phase or dimension.[4]

The Mystical Journey toward Unity with God

In her classic work *Mysticism*, English scholar Evelyn Underhill explains the traditional mystical journey to God, comprising the threefold pattern of purgation, illumination, and union, by expanding it to five successive phases as follows:

---

4. The distinction between False and True Self is discussed in chapter 2 below.

Spiritual and Developmental Models of Life

1. The *awakening* of the Self to consciousness of the Divine Reality. This experience, usually abrupt but well-marked, is accompanied by intense feelings of joy and exaltation. From a religious perspective, this awakening appears to be an intense form of the experience known as conversion or sanctification. Whereas the biological birth of the individual is to a small world controlled by deep-rooted instincts of self-preservation and self-enlargement, conversion enlarges the individual consciousness, bringing it into contact with a larger world of being. Conversion often results in a conviction of the nearness of God, coupled with the sense of a new life to be lived by the Self in correspondence with this new form of existence.

2. The *purgation* of the Self through discipline and mortification of all that stands in the way of its progress toward God. This phase, which involves the purification of the senses, is painful in nature, requiring great effort and commitment.

3. The *illumination* of the Self. Like the prisoners in Plato's "cave of illusion," the Self advances to this experience through contemplation. As Underhill notes, the experience of illumination is one mystics share with many seers and artists. While illumination brings an apprehension of the Absolute, those who experience this blissful state have not yet achieved true union with this Divine Presence.

4. The *purification* of the Self, known as the "dark night of the soul." Viewed as the final purification of the Self, this phase is also called the "mystic pain" or "mystic death." In this state, the consciousness that had experienced joy and bliss in illumination now suffers under an equally intense sense of Divine Absence. As in purgation, when the senses were cleansed and humbled, so now the purifying process is extended to the will. This is the "spiritual crucifixion" so often described by mystics, a desolation experienced when the Self fully surrenders its individuality and will. In this phase, the Self is utterly passive, asking and desiring nothing.

5. The *union* of the Self with the Absolute. In this phase, the Self does not merely apprehend the Divine, but is actually one with it. In this state of equilibrium, the seeker experiences the final goal of the spiritual quest. This phase, erroneously called ecstasy by some authorities, is characterized by peaceful joy, enhanced power, and intense certitude. While visions and ecstasies may be experienced in the illuminative

phase, such experiences seem to diminish rather than increase in frequency after the state of union has been achieved.

Unlike mystics of Eastern religions, who regard annihilation or reabsorption of the individual soul in the Infinite as the goal of the spiritual journey, Western Christian mystics describe the goal as "mystical marriage" or "deification," by which they mean not a passive state of non-being but an active way of life, resulting in passion for life and in service of God and others. For such mystics, the obstacle to unity is not consciousness in general but self-consciousness, the consciousness of the False Self or ego.[5]

Passion for life and for service of others characterized the unitive life of great organizers and leaders such as Hildegard of Bingen, Teresa of Ávila, John of the Cross, Francis of Assisi, Ignatius Loyola, George Fox, and Meister Eckhart, as well as of poets, prophets, and visionaries such as Mechtild of Magdeburg, Julian of Norwich, Joan of Arc, Catherine of Genoa, and Catherine of Siena. Indeed, as God's voice said to Catherine of Siena, "The soul enamored of My Truth never ceases to serve the whole world in general."[6] As the supreme Western mystics acknowledge, once the Self has established intimate communion with the Divine and reordered its inner life upon transcendent levels, it is impelled to abandon its spiritual solitude and resume, in transformed ways, its contact with the world in order to serve as the medium whereby the Divine Life flows toward others. In the mystical quest, the notion of spiritual retreat as preliminary to a return to fullness of life remains the true ideal of Christian spirituality in its highest development.

Spiritual and Psychological Approaches

Despite compatibility between spirituality and psychology, Christians need to resist the tendency to reduce spirituality to psychological terms. While there are similarities of interest and areas of overlap between spiritual and psychological realms, they represent fundamentally different disciplines. Psychological methods and attitudes are far more objective and tangible than their spiritual counterparts. To formulate too strict a separation, however, to divorce mind from spirit, is artificial and obstructive. We are human beings, with body, mind, and spirit all reflecting aspects of our unified

---

5. Underhill, *Mysticism*, 169–75.
6. Cited in Underhill, *Mysticism*, 173.

being or soul. To consider the spirit (the dynamic force of being) without addressing the mind is unhelpful, like caring for the mind while ignoring physical health. Thus, some kind of balanced attitude is required.

The most obvious difference between psychotherapy and spiritual formation is that the former focuses more on mental and emotional dimensions such as thoughts, feelings, and moods, while the latter focuses more precisely on spiritual issues such as prayer, religious experiences, and the sense of relationship to God. While some kind of balanced attitude is needed, we must beware the danger of collapsing mind, emotions, and relationships under the general rubric of spirituality. Likewise, spirituality must avoid focusing attention excessively on extrasensory psychic experiences or on dream analysis. In such cases, the means have surpassed the goal.

For people on the spiritual journey, the goal is not spiritual experience in itself. Exciting and dramatic experiences can actually distract us from our goal of constancy toward God. Gerald May makes this distinction in *Care of Mind, Care of Spirit*, his study on the psychiatric dimension of spiritual direction: "Although spiritual journeys often begin in the context of experience, and although experiences constitute major vehicles of insight, growth, support, and service along the way, the goal of the journey can never legitimately be experience itself. The goal is beyond experience, and has to do with our actually becoming who God means us to be and doing what God means us to do. Experiences can sometimes be a helpful means towards this end, and they can sometimes get in the way. But they are never the end in themselves."[7] Our task is not to trust experience but to trust God.

For those pursuing spiritual goals, it is a good rule of thumb to ask questions such as, "What does it mean to focus on God?" or "What things are preventing the working of the Holy Spirit in my life?" All human experiences can be said to be spiritual in the larger sense, but spirituality focuses most clearly on those areas that reveal the presence or leading of God in one's life. In spirituality, therefore, primary attention should be given to personal prayer life; to practices such as meditation and contemplation and other ways to simplify and slow things down; to awareness of God's presence, absence, or callings; to experiences of fundamental meaning; to personal longing for God; and to the multiplicity of factors that seem to help or hinder fullness of living in God's presence.

In general, psychotherapy encourages effective living, and its values often reflect prevailing values in the surrounding culture. For example,

---

7. May, *Care of Mind*, 38.

psychotherapeutic approaches focus on helping patients achieve autonomous mastery over self and circumstance, whereas spirituality seeks liberation from attachments and self-surrender to the discerned power and will of God. While stricter forms of psychiatry view the physician as healer and the patient as client, in more humanistic psychotherapies, therapist and client form a healing team together.

In spiritual formation, however, the true healer, nurturer, sustainer, and liberator is God, and the disciple is a hopeful channel of grace. In their spiritual pursuit, seekers must reject two extremes, the temptation to play God (that is, substituting personal mastery for surrender to divine will), and the risk of apathy, whereby seekers avoid their own graced potential for action by refraining from doing anything at all. If examined closely, both extremes reflect excessive willfulness, the former by aggrandizing personal power, and the latter by restricting it. The one denies the transcendence of God; the other denies God's immanence and human responsiveness to God.

Questions for Discussion and Reflection

In addition to the questions listed at the end of the preface, answer the following questions, writing your answers in a journal. If you are in a group study, be prepared to share your answers with those in the group.

1. If most humans pattern their lives after some model, which pattern seems most helpful to you—biological, social, psychological, moral, existential, or religious? If none of the above, is there another model or pattern you prefer? If so, which? If not, why not?

2. Is there a period or time in your life you consider your prime or your best? If so, when did it occur, and can such a period or experience lie in your future? Explain your answer.

3. Was there a point in your life when you acquired a clear sense of morality? If so, did you ever question or rebel against these principles? Explain your answer. If not, why not?

4. At this point in your life, are you still following a ser of borrowed or acquired "life commandments," or are your moral principles and guidelines essentially your own? Explain your answer.

Spiritual and Developmental Models of Life

5. At this point in your life, do you consider your moral principles to based more on pragmatic ideals or on an external or inherited religious or moral code of beliefs and obligations? Explain your answer.

6. Did you ever go through a period of spiritual doubt or confusion? If so, how did it affect your understanding of God? Of scripture? Of organized religion?

7. Do you consider yourself to be in the first or second half of your spiritual journey? Explain your answer.

8. Of the four spiritual paths in Hinduism, which do you find most attractive, and which best describes your spiritual path to this point? Explain your answer.

9. I your own words, explain the meaning and the validity of the phenomenon Kierkegaard described as the "teleological suspension of the ethical."

10. Assess the validity of the model the author calls the "five halves of life," and indicate the phase that best describes your current spiritual state. Explain your answer.

11. Assess the validity of the author's statement that some form of awakening or spiritual conversion is (or may be) foundational for second half of life spirituality.

12. Explain the meaning and assess the validity of the Christian mystical notion that describes the goal of the spiritual journey as "deification."

13. Explain and assess the need for believers to resist the tendency to reduce spirituality to psychological terms.

2

Holistic Pain

SUFFERING IS A UNIVERSAL condition, and there is no way to avoid it. There is hardly a time in any family when someone is not experiencing significant illness or when that family has not experienced the loss of a loved one. Life and death are part of a continuum, and whatever is alive is moving toward death. In some cases death comes suddenly, but generally speaking, all living things are in the process of dying. Pain, suffering, and loss are part of that process.

Illness seems to affect children and the aged more than the rest of the population, and for obvious reasons. Overall, children are acquiring an effective immune system, and childhood illnesses benefit that process. Likewise, the elderly are more susceptible to illness because their immune system is less functional than before. People with healthy genes, a good immune system, and a positive mental attitude often seem to thrive; others are not so fortunate.

There are things most of us can do to mitigate the effects of suffering and pain, such as diet and exercise, but that is not the subject of this chapter. Our focus will be on accepting pain and suffering when they come, not by welcoming them or by exaggerating their effects through hypochondria, but by using their mentoring power beneficially.

In Old Testament times, suffering due to sickness and tragedy was believed to be caused by sin. People either assumed or were taught that suffering was God's punishment for disobeying divine laws (see Deut 28:27–28). Of course, this belief is not that of present-day Judaism. However, even within the Old Testament we find objections to the notion that sickness is

Holistic Pain

the result of sin. The strongest protest is found in the book of Job, which provides three explanations for suffering. The first attempt to explain suffering appears in the prologue: (a) *innocent suffering arises from arbitrary divine decisions.* Job is but a pawn in a heavenly challenge, and humans are unwitting victims. Job's friends propose a different interpretation: (b) *suffering is due to sin*; hence, Job's suffering is deserved. Job's own experience, and the reader's knowledge of the situation, invalidate this conclusion. (c) *The Creator of all things must be the cause and source of suffering.* According to Job, humans suffer because God is capricious and unreliable. In the divine speeches, God merely ignores Job's questions, changing the subject from Job's pain to the creation of the cosmos.

In the past, the customary way of understanding suffering, as punishment for sin, seems validated by Job's "repentance" in 42:6. Recent biblical and theological study has led to more viable explanations, including viewing suffering as:

1. *A test of one's character and integrity.* The prologue itself tells us that God allowed Job's misfortunes to befall him so that Job's integrity might be tested (2:3). Elsewhere in the Bible God is said to test individuals, such as when Abraham was told to sacrifice his son Isaac (Gen 22:1). While experiences certainly test our character, we must add that in Job's case he never regarded his misfortune as a test.

2. *A source of moral discipline.* In the book of Job, Elihu claims that pain and sickness sometimes act as warning against sin and as a defense against pride and complacency (33:15–33).

3. *Vicarious suffering.* This view is depicted in the Suffering Servant poems in the book of Isaiah, particularly in 52:13—53:12, interpreted by Jews as reference to Jewish Diaspora experience and by Christians as a reference to Christ's atoning sacrifice on the cross. Such suffering is said to be an instrument whereby God's will is accomplished, bringing blessing to the world.

4. *A place of encounter with God.* As in Job's case, God can be experienced either as absent or as particularly close and available in suffering and pain.

5. *An impersonal result of universal sin.* In the Bible, this is how death seems to be understood, as a sort of karmic effect of cosmic rebellion and human wrongdoing (Rom 6:23). The Christian doctrine of

"original sin," which views Adam's sin as having infected all humans, is sometimes introduced as a variant of this explanation.

6. *A mystery.* Innocent suffering is simply beyond human comprehension. Ultimately no one can give Job an adequate explanation for his suffering. Only God knows, though people of faith expect that one day all will become clear.

In biblical times, Greeks and Romans held a traditional understanding of sickness, viewing it as the direct result of the anger of the gods against human beings who had violated natural laws. People born blind, for example, or who contracted diseases such as leprosy, were considered cursed by God and were shunned by most people. This idea was propagated by the majority of Christians throughout history, and it continues to be held in some circles to this day.

Although some illness may be caused by moral and religious failure, we must note that in his ministry Jesus contravened all notions that God brings sickness or pestilence upon people because of divine wrath. Jesus' healing ministry embodied the exact antithesis of this idea. Before healing people, Jesus did not inquire whether they were bad or good or whether they had repented or were reforming. He loved people as they were, and desired only to help them out of their misery.

Another idea current in Christian circles today is that God sends illness or deprivation upon believers for their good, or to accomplish divine ends. Speaking of the value of illness, they sometimes point to the "thorn in the flesh" passage in 2 Corinthians 12:7–10, where Paul speaks of a malady in his life sent to keep him humble. The passage includes the oft-quoted words, "My grace is sufficient for you, for (my) power is made perfect through weakness." When we examine this passage, however, we note that Paul is not attributing the malady to God, nor is he indicating that it was a good thing. Rather, the malady "came as a messenger of Satan" to keep Paul humble. Self-centeredness itself is a malady, when it prevents us from being God-centered. No doubt God would have preferred Paul without his pride *and* his thorn, but the point of the passage is that suffering for one's faith can bring God glory: "Therefore I am content with weaknesses, insults, hardships, persecution, and calamities for the sake of Christ; for whenever I am weak, then I am strong" (2 Cor 12:10).

Ultimately, it is a travesty to blame God for suffering. While a loving God can use the afflictions of evil to work good, a loving God does not send evil. Some suffering redeems, but most suffering destroys. God wills life, not death; healing, not disease. The essence of God's manifesto regarding good is found in the Beatitudes (Matt 5:3–12). There we learn that God's desire is to bless and not curse, to grant wholeness and not deprivation.

One of the greatest lessons I have learned as a Christian is that nothing befalls us without first going through God. In other words, when we suffer, God suffers with us. Perhaps for this reason, Brother Lawrence wrote that God seems "nearer to us, and more effectually present with us, in sickness than in health."[1] Often, when things go well, we become self-sufficient and oblivious of God, but when illness and tragedy strike, we recognize our vulnerability and our need of help. The good news is that God is especially near at such times, willing and able to help. As environmentalist Wendell Berry once said, speaking at a coffeehouse on a dreary December day, "It gets darker and darker, and then Jesus is born." Annie Dillard pushed the imagery deeper when she writes, "If you want to look at the stars . . . darkness is required."

Christianity is the only faith that looks squarely at the almost limitless extent of human agony and suffering, takes it seriously, and then offers meaning, redemption, and victory. This view is best depicted in Jesus' resurrection. The essential message of the teaching, life, death, and resurrection of Jesus is that evil and death have been defeated, and that we share in that victory. As the incarnation makes clear, God is with us in our joys and in our trials. Christianity neither ignores human agony nor dismisses it as irrelevant.

Essential to the biblical doctrine of creation is the notion that God created human beings for fellowship. Love created human beings, and that love remains with God's creatures for the long haul, through thick and thin. As the apostle Paul proclaimed, "If God is for us, who is against us? . . . . Who will separate us from the love of Christ? Will hardship, or distress, or persecution, or famine, or nakedness, or peril, or sword? . . . No, in all these things we are more than conquerors through him who loved us. For I am convinced that neither death, nor life, nor angels, nor rulers, nor things present, nor things to come, nor powers, nor height, nor depth, nor anything else in all creation, will be able to separate us from the love of God in Christ Jesus" (Rom 8:31–39).

There are many ways we can keep in touch with the Easter victory, ways of opening our lives to the spiritual dimension. These include prayer, sacrament, meditation, and contemplation. There are also qualities such as

---

1. Lawrence, *Practice of the Presence*, 55.

faith, humility, and courage that are central to the victorious and fulfilled life. However, there is yet another way to encounter the deep truths of the gospel. We can make contact with the risen Christ through a language far older than logical or conceptual thinking—through the faculty of imagination, the language of images, feeling, and love. Imagination can lead to atom bombs and can be used for evil or escapist purposes. However, imagination can also open us to the realm of the divine, to the loving, conquering, resurrected Jesus, who is able to sympathize with our weakness because he was tested as we are, perfected through suffering (Heb 2:10; 4:15).

Creative Suffering

Life is beautiful, but it is also hard—for all human beings, but even harder in misfortune or deprivation. While life is harder for some than for others, in everyone's life there is a mixture of privilege and deprivation. Every event bears pain and joy; our response determines our growth, physically, emotionally, and spiritually.

In *Creative Suffering*, Swiss physician Paul Tournier demonstrates persuasively that many of the world's greatest statesmen, religious leaders, creative artists, and physicians suffered great loss and deprivation in their early years. Deprivation, it seems—whether due to failure, loss, accident, bereavement, or infirmity—has the power to transform lives. This is true not only in the lives of individuals but also of nations. Sociologists indicate that the most propitious regions for the development of civilization are not the tropics, or areas where the weather is most favorable, but rather those regions with the greatest contrast in climate. Such extremes release a surge of creativity, and it is this creative reaction to life's extremes that influences change, vitality, and development. Consider also what happened to the two most important countries defeated in World War Two, Germany and Japan. Both responded with prodigious development, as epitomized by Emperor Hirohito when he announced surrender: "We must now accept the unacceptable, and surmount the insurmountable." A nation's value, like a person's, can be measured not so much by success as by how it responds to failure or defeat.

When it comes to suffering and pain, most important is not what happens to us but how we respond. Though not always welcome, pain has proven to be a great mentor, valuable for its transformative potential.

Holistic Pain

The following list represents some reasons I am grateful for pain, whether physical, emotional, and spiritual:

1. Pain creates perspective.
2. Pain builds character.
3. Pain produces compassion.
4. Pain instills hope.
5. Pain enhances listening skills.
6. Pain increases self-awareness.
7. Pain brings us closer to God.
8. Pain makes us appreciate better times.
9. Pain makes us feel alive.
10. Pain lets us know things could be worse.

As I learned recently while recovering from a prolonged ailment, when exercising an injured or debilitated area of the body, it helps to focus on the parts of the body that are working well, and not solely on the parts that are incapacitated. Likewise, speaking spiritually, when you suffer deprivation, focus on blessings rather than on woes.

Positive, creative, reactions to suffering enhance one's life; negative, resistant, reactions stunt it. Like a game of chess, a single move can change the entire game. Think also of the "snowball effect": every positive reaction renews hope and enhances progress, and every negative reaction paves the way for further defeat. Two beneficial outcomes exist in every illness: the possibility of healing and of personal growth. In both cases, the attitude of faith makes a huge difference. Patients, generally speaking, think only of healing, and that is normal. When you are in need of healing, go to the doctors, where you will get professional help. But go also to God, for while doctors seek to heal the whole by healing the part, God, it seems, heals the parts by healing the whole. All healing, however, ultimately comes from God, since God is creator of the natural as well as the supernatural, the physical as well as the spiritual.

In *On Death and Dying*, Swiss psychiatrist Elisabeth Kübler-Ross described the five stages in acceptance of grief or loss. At first there is shock, when a patient learns or assesses the severity of illness or the death of a loved one. Shock is accompanied by denial—unwillingness to accept the loss. This is followed by the "bargaining stage," as if the patient could placate fate or God through submission. During the fourth stage, the feeling of helplessness leads to withdrawal and sometimes to harmful self-medication. Finally, after a long pilgrimage, the sick person or mourner arrives at peaceful acceptance.

With variations, we can see Kübler-Ross's stages in those who advance to old age—some people remain in good health until the end, but most people experience physical and mental decline. For those who age graciously, that is, who reach the stage of acceptance, the greatest factor is faith. Retirement and old age are forms of deprivation—loss of prestige, of social relationships, of routine—but also opportunities for personal growth. Those who find meaning in retirement generally find it through creative transformation; these people become embedded in the moment, living mindfully. This requires new values and fresh inspiration.

When Jesus spoke of discipleship, he talked about renunciation and loss of the old self. His words ring true, because he accepted the cross, despite undergoing inner struggle at Gethsemane (Matt 26:36). Struggling with loss and deprivation is part of discipleship, because every trial brings us closer to faithfulness and thus to Christ. It is in suffering that we perceive his nearness, his presence, his participation in our lives. In the end, it is not simply human acceptance of suffering or loss that matters, but God's love that makes acceptance possible and leads us forward. According to Tournier, "I believe we can face everything when we believe we are loved."[2]

Like most families, mine was not spared traumatic, life-changing calamities. At the age of ten, my father lost an eye in a sledding accident, and at the age of forty-eight, while in the prime of her life, my mother contracted cancer. It was breast cancer, quite possibly a woman's worst fear, and it struck while my mother was fully engaged in a care-giving ministry for the God she loved and served. A mastectomy was performed, and after several months of improving health, she discovered another lump forming in her other breast. Was this spreading of cancer an indication that her ministry, perhaps even her life, was at an end, or was this experience a "wound of love," like the limp that the Old Testament patriarch Jacob received when he wrestled with God, when he received a new name (Israel) and a renewed promise for himself and his posterity?

This event came at a time when my parents experienced a deepening of their faith and an enlarging of their ministry. My mother would go on

---

2. Tournier, *Creative Suffering*, 90.

Holistic Pain

to live forty additional years as a cancer survivor. My father became ordained to the gospel ministry in 1966, two years before his retirement, and he spent the next twenty-five years teaching himself Greek and Hebrew, eventually reading the entire Bible in the original languages, something few seminary graduates or Bible scholars have accomplished. And he did this with the use of one eye.

As a young adult, discouraged and downhearted, I confronted my parents with a litany of doomsday scenarios. Without a moment's hesitation, my mother responded out of the reservoir of hope that had fueled her faith during times when her life was at risk, particularly as a missionary in Colombia—the Syria, Iraq, and Afghanistan of its day in the sense of deep sectarian violence and conflict and the place that inspired Fidel Castro to become a militant Marxist. My mother's response as I confronted my fears was hopeful and unwavering: "The best is yet to come." She knew, quoting Corrie ten Boom, the Dutch Christian who survived the concentration camps where she was sent for harboring Jews during World War II, that "There is no pit so deep that God's love is not deeper still."

Illness has taught me a great deal about myself, about God's elusive nature, and about how better to tap into divine resources. Undoubtedly, there is more learning and growing ahead, probably more than I can achieve in one short lifetime, making the notion of eternal life increasingly plausible. While increasing my hope for healing, this illness has increased my patience and given me a deeper appreciation for family and strangers, in whom I increasingly find the image of God. With Anne Lamott, I am discovering that "when God is about to do something wonderful, God always starts with a hardship, and when God is going to do something amazing, God starts with an impossibility."[3]

Near the end of his life, Friedrich von Hügel (1852–1925), one of the most original theologians of his era, wrote these words to his niece, fittingly summarize life: "Remember, no joy without suffering, no patience without trial, no humility without humiliation, no life without death."[4] At the age of eighteen, sickened with typhus fever and left practically deaf, he embarked on a theological career. While he spent most of his life as a Catholic layman dedicated to theological and philosophical writing, at the age of forty he met the Abbé Huvelin, a distinguished spiritual director serving in a Parisian parish. Through his influence, von Hügel experienced a profound

---

3. Lamott, *Plan B*, 33–34.
4. Steere, *Spiritual Counsel and Letters of von Hügel*, 34.

spiritual transformation that led him from his intellectual pursuits into the field of spiritual counseling, and it was as a guide and counselor that he made his greatest contribution. Because of his deafness, much of his counsel occurred by correspondence, through the mail. Many of his letters exist in published form. Among those who sought his direction was Evelyn Underhill, distinguished in intellectual circles for her books on mysticism.

What von Hügel learned at eighteen from his own spiritual director, Father Raymond Hocking, when he decided on a career in theology, he applied as a spiritual counselor: "You want to grow in virtue, to serve God, to love Christ? Well, you will grow in and attain these things if you will make them a slow and sure, but utterly real, mountain-step plod and ascent, willing to have to camp for weeks in spiritual desolation, darkness, and emptiness at different stages in your march and growth. All demand for constant light, all attempt at eliminating or minimizing the cross and trial, is so much soft folly and puerile trifling."[5] These words reflect what Jesus taught his followers about the cost of discipleship: "If any want to become my followers, let them deny themselves and take up their cross and follow me. For those who want to save their life will lose it, and those who lose their life for my sake and for the sake of the gospel, will save it" (Mark 8:34–35). A more realistic description of the Christian spiritual journey has not been recorded. But the story does not end here, for Jesus also taught his followers that wherever they go, he would accompany them (Matt 28:20). Those who are yoked to Jesus experience exhilaration and joy daily, even in times of trial, for Christ's burden is light (Matt 11:30).

While most suffering and deprivation is borne individually, with the help of others, some deprivation may be redemptive or vicarious. In ancient times, the people of Israel viewed the Babylonian exile as divine punishment for social injustice and religious unfaithfulness. That, at least, is the interpretation given in Israel's prophetic literature. However, an alternative interpretation arose, based on the book of Job. According to this view, Job is Israel, and the story of Job an allegorical account of Israel's experiences during the Babylonian exile. This interpretation views Israel as an innocent victim, and the exile as the story of servant Israel's vicarious suffering on behalf of the nations of the world, including Israel's unrighteous enemies. Such an interpretation became useful to Christianity's characterization of Jesus as the Suffering Servant of the Lord, as the one who's suffering would bring salvation not only to Israel but also to the Gentiles (see Isa 49:1–7 and

---

5. Steere, *Spiritual Counsel and Letters of von Hügel*, 4.

53:1–12). According to Isaiah 53, the Servant's suffering is not for his own wrongdoing but is the way he brings his people to salvation.

While there are many ways to understand suffering, one is to view it as having redemptive value. In this perspective, one's suffering is offered as a prayer for the common good. In redemptive suffering, we stand with others in their pain and suffering. There is an active and a passive role here. The passive side involves those trials that enter our daily lives. These can be minor or tragic. Sometimes they come through disobedience or poor choices. Other times we are caught in the riptide of a good world gone bad—a bad economy that endangers our life savings, unemployment, an illness or accident that changes our life forever. When we suffer things for which we are not responsible and over which we have no control, we are to endure them patiently, putting our trust in God. We can also offer our sorrows and suffering as gifts to God, asking that they be used to heal the world. The active side of suffering involves standing in solidarity with people in need, voluntarily taking into ourselves the griefs and sorrows of others in order to set them free.

Death and Resurrection of the Self

Modern Western society presents a rosy picture: the journey ahead is upward and onward. You can be successful, and you can do it by yourself. Jesus, however, presents us with a different model, that of death and resurrection—a pattern of renewal, of daily dying to self. This leaves us with an important question, "How much False Self are we willing to shed to find our True Self?" The True Self is who you are from the beginning, in the heart of God, the "face we had before we were born," as the Zen masters say. In this light, Swiss psychiatrist Carl Jung offered a momentous insight: "Life is a luminous pause between two great mysteries, which themselves are one." In his inimitable way, Irish poet William Butler Yates probed deeper when he wrote, "Many times man lives and dies between his two eternities."

Life's ultimate adventure, its grandest game and greatest challenge, is the spiritual transformation (rebirth) of the self. As I discuss in many of my writings on spirituality, the role of authentic spirituality is letting go of the False Self, one's incomplete self trying to pass for one's True Self. Our True Self, our inherent soul, is that part of us that sees reality accurately, truthfully. It is divine breath passing through us, dwelling with us. Our False Self is the egoic self that is limited and constantly changing. It masquerades as true and permanent but in reality is passing, tentative, and fearful of change. It is that part of us that will eventually die. The role of true spirituality, of mature religion, is to help speed up this process of dying to the False Self.

Not surprisingly, we cannot accomplish—or even understand—what we have not been told to look for or to expect. This staggering change of perspective—that our ego is not our True Self—is what Jesus came to convey to humanity. It led Thomas Merton, the Trappist monk who first suggested use of the term False Self, to his radical rediscovery of the meaning of Jesus' teaching that his followers must lose their False Self in order to discover their True Self (see Mark 8:35).

Unfortunately, many traditionalists remain quite rigid in their thinking because they have been taught that faith requires adherence to the religious status quo, and with it unquestioned obedience to the guardians of tradition. Such people are often moral and productive—even model citizens—but they underrate the centrality of paradox or mystery to the faith traditions they espouse. When many religious practitioners observe rituals faithfully without experiencing spiritual transformation at any deep level, religion becomes a duty that actually prevents transformation from taking place. This has been going on for centuries, and in all faith traditions.

Mature religion talks about the death of any notion of a separate, False Self, while recognizing that only a deep security in a larger love will give us the courage to do that. The True Self can let go because it is secure at its core. Our False Self, however, does not let go easily. As Jesus and other great spiritual teachers made clear, there is a self that must be found and another that must be renounced. This teaching is found in each gospel (see Matt 10:39; 16:25; Mark 8:35; Luke 9:24), but is central to John's gospel, where it is coupled with "dying to the self": "unless a grain of wheat falls into the earth and dies, it remains just a single grain; but if it dies, it bears much fruit" (John 12:24). Hence, "those who love their life lose it [that is, their False Self], and those who hate their life [their False Self] in this world will keep it [their True Self] for eternal life" (John 12:25; see also 1 Cor 15:36–37, 42).

In one way or another, almost all religions say that we must die before we die—and then we will know what dying means, and what it does not mean. What it means, of course, is the relinquishment of selfish, possessive living, of egoic existence. The ego self is the self before death. Some form of death—psychological, spiritual, relational, or physical—is the only way we will loosen our ties to our small and separate False Self. Only then does it return in a new shape, which we call the soul, the True Self, or the Risen Christ.

There are four major splits from reality that we have all made in varying degrees to create our False Self:

- We split our mind from our body and soul, and live in our minds
- We split life from death and try to live without any "death"
- We split from our shadow self and pretend to be our idealized self
- We split ourselves from other selves and try to live apart, superior, and separate[6]

Each of these illusions must be overcome, either in this world or at the moment of physical death. Spirituality, pure and simple, is overcoming these splits from Reality. Anything less than the death of the False Self is inadequate religion. The False Self must die for the True Self to live, or, as Jesus put it, "If I do not go, the Advocate [the Holy Spirit] will not come to you" (John 16:7). Theologically speaking, what this verse is telling us is that Jesus (a good person) still had to die for the Christ (the universal presence) to arise. This is the pattern of transformation, where the letting go of the original indispensable self results in the arrival of a better reality.

Our True Self sees truthfully and will live forever. Our False Self is constantly changing and will eventually die. Our False Self is our necessary warm-up, our ego part that establishes our separate identity, especially in the first half of life. It is our incomplete self trying to pass for our whole self. The role of true spirituality, of mature religion, is to help speed up this process of dying to the False Self. Whatever one calls it, true spirituality is the form of living embodied by Jesus and taught by the Buddha. Such calm, egoless approach to life is invariably characteristic of people at the highest levels of doing and loving in all cultures and religions. These are the ones we call sages or holy ones.

Sometimes the end is the beginning, and the beginning points toward the end. As many poets and mystics have noted, the One Great Mystery is revealed at the beginning of our lives and forever beckons us toward its full realization. Many of us cannot let go of this implanted promise. Some call this homing device the soul, some call it the indwelling Holy Spirit, and others think of it as nostalgia or dreamtime. Whatever we call it, we cannot ignore it. It calls us both backward and forward, to our foundation and our future at the same time. The soul lives in such eternally deep time.

---

6. Rohr, *Diamond*, 29.

Speaking of this mystery, Richard Rohr notes that we are called forward by "a kind of deep homesickness," an inherent dissatisfaction that comes from our original and radical union with God.[7] Like loneliness, sadness, and depression, sickness, loss, and deprivation can serve as beacons to light our way home. One of the reasons the *Wizard of Oz* has such lasting appeal is because Dorothy is guided forward to Oz and back to Kansas by her constant love and desire for home. Restlessness and dissatisfaction in life can serve as pointers to our destiny in God. The moment that we find ourselves in the presence of God is the moment we also find ourselves inside God.

The end was planted in us at the beginning, and it gnaws at us until we get there freely and consciously. Suffering, tragedy, and all episodes of loss in our lives are potentially sacramental. As Carl Jung put it, "when you stumble and fall, there you find pure gold." God hides, and is found, precisely in the depths of everything, especially so in the deep fathoming of our pain, suffering, weakness, and failure. This "something real" is what all the world religions point to when they speak of heaven, nirvana, bliss, or enlightenment. Their only mistake is to push it off into the next world. "If heaven comes later, it is because it is first of all now."[8]

How does God operate? We really don't know. But so many have encountered God in their weakness that we realize God's strength is God's ability to be patient, to refrain from overt use of power. From our perspective, then, we can say that God is a god of weakness, acting as much by persuasion as by direct action.

In tragedy and sickness, we are no longer in charge. That is good news, because all attempts to engineer or plan our own enlightenment are doomed to failure, since they are ego driven. The ego's job is to protect the status quo, so failure and humiliation force us to look beyond our comfort zones. Thus, we must stumble and fall. We must get out of the driver's seat for a while or we will never learn how to give up control to our soul's True Guide.

If we desire to grow spiritually, eventually some idea, event, or relationship will enter our life that we are not equipped to handle, using our present skill set. Richard Rohr calls such a situation a "stumbling stone," an event that causes you to leave your comfort zone in life.[9] Often such an experience involves physical or mental suffering. In this case, suffering

---

7. The material in this segment is adapted from Rohr, *Falling Upward*, 65–96.
8. Rohr, *Falling Upward*, 95.
9. Rohr, *Falling Upward.*, 68.

will not solve any problem mechanically so much as it discloses the chronic problem in our lives, the refusal of our ego to let go. In such cases, suffering has a mentoring role, that of opening up new spaces within us for learning and loving. Francis of Assisi noted that when he kissed the leper, "what had been nauseating to me became sweetness and life." He marked that moment as his conversion, as the defining moment in his life, when he tasted his own insufficiency and began drawing from a different source.[10]

Courage: Our Finest Hour

Is it possible for those victimized by deprivation or great misfortune, such as the physically and mentally disadvantaged, to discover in that experience creative energy? Tournier answers that question affirmatively, but only if two conditions are present: (a) they must find a task in life and the tools to perform it adequately, and (b) they must learn to tap into their inherent sense of courage.

Lengthy suffering requires a great deal of courage, the kind of courage that cannot be taught, but rather is caught. This kind of courage is exemplified in Winston Churchill's 1940 "Finest Hour" speech before Parliament, uttered shortly before the Battle of Britain began. In that speech, Churchill galvanized all of Great Britain by offering only blood, toil, tears, and sweat. It was not forced measures he demanded, however, for it was his own courage that was on display.

Sometimes sufferers display extraordinary courage—even joy—in the face of adversity. What is the explanation? In many cases it is the result of their spiritual condition, for courage belongs to the realm of the Spirit; as such, it comes from an inexhaustible supply. Like all things spiritual, the more we use it, the more we have. Doctor Tournier tells the story of one of his colleagues in medicine who for years had been treating a woman for anemia, without ever achieving a hemoglobin count of more than 68 percent. One day he found that it was over 80 percent. He asked her what had happened since her last visit, and she replied that she "had found faith." Because it is spiritual, courage comes from God. And when God calls us to make a courageous decision, God also gives the strength to bear the consequences.

Why is courage necessary in misfortune? Because in facing misfortune courageously we suffer far less than if we lapse into despair. Will power, however, is not enough. Behind courage is an attitude we call creativity.

10. Rohr, *Falling Upward.*, 69–70.

Holistic Happiness

Behind all deprivation and suffering are opportunities for creativity. While it is not suffering that makes a person grow, one does not grow without suffering. While suffering may not be creative in itself, we are scarcely ever creative without suffering.

How is it that creativity results from deprivation? The answer comes from biological evolution, which teaches us that a succession of random errors in the duplication of the genetic code is the key to the evolution of living species. Marital conflict illustrates this process. Through a long series of small conflicts husbands and wives adapt to one another, producing a relationship that is more complex, productive, and solid than the simplistic relationship of a honeymoon. Those couples, however, who lack the courage to confront one another, who avoid conflict for the sake of peace, often become strangers to each other, allowing repressed grudges to erupt with catastrophic consequences.

How consoling it is to discover that we learn from our mistakes, and that we owe the wonderful diversity of living species to lapses in DNA—mistakes in copying the genetic code. How interesting that physics, the most scientific of disciplines, is the one to discover the discontinuous, random, and unforeseeable side of nature, of which all we can measure is its probability. This, then, is God's method, the art of using random mutations in order to accomplish the divine plan, akin to how God uses evil for our salvation. How comforting to know that God uses not only our strength but also our weakness to guide us.

The nutcracker illustrates our thesis perfectly. The shell of the nut represents the protective refuge that gradually becomes hardened by the routine of good health, vitality, and well-being. The shell encloses the tender fruit of creativity, newness, and change. Nutcrackers are those deprivations that disturb the ongoing process of life, fossilized in routine. The breaking of the nut is the calamity that strikes us. Which of us has not felt broken by some particular painful event? But there is another important side to this. The hard shell is the rigid, fixed framework of the genetic code, the habits, prejudices, and behavioral patterns that imprison us.[11]

The maxim, "history is but a succession of irremediable disasters," speaks of the cracking of the nut. Nevertheless, the nut cannot break open of itself. This, then, is our lesson, that what disturbs our lives, puts us out, irritates and makes us suffer, is what makes growth and development possible, on condition, of course, that we are not destroyed by it.

---

11. Tournier, *Creative Suffering*, 129–31.

Holistic Pain

Think about what happens when calamity strikes. When something is broken in us, how do we respond? Generally by asking ourselves questions that tend to get forgotten in the routine of ordinary life—about the meaning of existence, suffering, pain, and death. Our materialistic world does not teach us how to cope with adversity, so we need to fall back on our creativity and imagination. Creativity has always been there, hidden, blocked by convention, but present within, the gift of God. The biblical writer expressed this aptly in Genesis 1:27: "So God created humankind in his image." Because God is Creator, to be in God's image is to be endowed with creativity. Hence our need for adventure, for newness and growth. Break the nut and you will discover the potential inside.

Questions for Discussion and Reflection

In addition to the questions listed at the end of the preface, answer the following questions, writing your answers in a journal. If you are in a group study, be prepared to share your answers with those in the group.

1. What role have illness or death played in your life or in your family's life? In these situations, how did you cope with loss and tragedy?

2. In dealing with pain, illness, and loss, have you been able to view them as beneficial mentors, or simply as negative, overwhelming, and undesirable experiences? Explain your answer.

3. Do you tend to view suffering, disease, and tragedy in your life as punishment for sin (moral and religious failure), as the result of poor choices or decisions, as means to accomplish divine ends, or simply as random events? Explain your answer.

4. Can you agree with those who view pain, suffering, and tragedy as opportunities for encounter with God? Has this even been your experience? Explain your answer.

5. In practical terms, explain the meaning of the resurrection of Jesus (the Easter victory) in your life. How does this doctrine or event influence, benefit, or expand you self- understanding, how you cope with life, and your hope for the future?

6. After reading this chapter, what die you learn about "creative suffering"?

7. In dealing with suffering and loss, can you agree with holocaust survivor Corrie ten Boom that "there is no pit so deep that God's love is not deeper still"? Explain your answer.

8. Respond to the notion that suffering can have vicarious or redemptive value.

9. Assess the validity of the notion that humans possess both a False and a True Self, and that life's greatest adventure is the spiritual transformation of one's "self."

10. Explain your understanding of the author's statement, "suffering, tragedy, and all episodes of loss in our lives are potentially sacramental."

11. After reading this chapter, what did you learn about the role of courage and creativity in times of suffering and deprivation?

3

Holistic Healing

HUMANS HAVE LONG SOUGHT the fountain of youth, the key to longevity, lasting happiness, and well-being, and not many things interest modern humans quite as much as their health. They not only talk about it—in public as well as in private—but they spend a great deal of energy on it. In the United States alone, hundreds of billions of dollars are spent to preserve health and prolong life. One of life's greatest lessons is that finding and preserving health, happiness, and well-being requires moderation and stability, achieved by maintaining equilibrium between action and rest, adventure and caution, stress and relaxation, success and failure, joy and sorrow.

While institutional religious commitment has fallen dramatically in the twenty-first century, religious beliefs, much of them aggressively conservative, have experienced a resurgence. Unlike their forebears, however, most people are now as absorbed in staying alive and healthy as their ancestors were in preparing for life after death. Even when the zest for living is gone, taking care of life in the here and now seems almost an obsession. It still does not occur to many people that spirituality might have some influence on the matter of mental and physical health, even though many medical professionals are suggesting this very idea.

Ironically, while the twentieth century saw the growth in psychological healing, primarily through the professions of psychiatry and clinical psychology, and while may physicians in other areas of medicine have come to realize that many physical illnesses have psychic roots as well as physical ones, during that same period, there was an actual decline among traditional clergy in approaching physical or mental healing through religious or spiritual means. With the exception of Pentecostals, some Independents, and Catholics, who treat healing sacramentally, traditional Protestant churches and seminaries ignore and in many cases dismiss religious or spiritual healing with scorn. It is true that religious groups build hospitals and medical centers, but this does not differ from any other act of charity or compassion.

How different from the ministry of Jesus and the apostles, a healing ministry that continued practically unbroken for the first thousand years of the church's life. The about-face in Christian belief and practice regarding spiritual healing can be traced to the tenth century, when the service of unction for healing was gradually transformed into extreme unction. That period saw the sacrament for healing become a rite of passage for dying, a change in emphasis from enhancing life in the present to rescuing individuals for the next life and speeding them quickly and easily into it. This held true to an even greater extent among Protestants, who dismissed such sacramental practices as superstition and who developed a rationale to show why healing does not and should not take place as a function of Christianity.

Eventually, Protestants developed four different but overlapping views of spiritual healing. First, they emphasized the materialistic notion that human bodies can be cared for adequately by medical and physical means alone, and that religious help is secondary at best. Next, they came to view sickness as God's direct and disciplinary gift. Another approach was that of dispensationalism, which espoused the belief that ministries such as healing are no longer valid, as they had been established by God only to help get the church established. Finally came the view, expressed by Liberal Protestants and secular thinkers, which denied the existence of a supernatural agency that could break into the autonomous physical realm ruled by natural law. Taken together, these views constitute a strong case against spiritual healing.

It is surprising to find how much Jesus differed from this sort of thinking, and how central was his religious concern for the physical and mental welfare of the sick, suffering, and infirm. As we see clearly in the gospels, Jesus came to the men and women of his day to heal their bodies and minds along with their souls, for in his understanding, these work together and belong together. As study of the historical Jesus shows, the interest Jesus demonstrated in the physical and mental health of human being was greater than that of any other leader or religious system from Moses through Confucius, or from Hinduism and Buddhism to Islam. There is no doubt what Jesus thought of the value of healing our minds and bodies or about the way he put it into practice. The source material found in the New Testament is clear and consistent. Forty-one distinct instances of physical and mental healing are recorded in the four gospels (there are seventy-two accounts in all, including duplications), but this by no means represents the total. Many of these references summarize the healings of large numbers of people. Those described in detail are simply the more dramatic instances of this activity of Jesus—by all accounts an extensive healing ministry.

The same held true for the followers of Jesus in the early church. It is clear that Jesus sent his disciples out to continue his healing ministry (Mark 6:7–13; Matt 10:5–10; Luke 9:1–6). As we note in the book of Acts, those who received the Holy Spirit were expected to become healing channels of God's love, as Jesus had been. Jesus' ministry of healing is certainly in line with the constant emphasis in his teachings upon compassion and caring about one's neighbor. Certainly this is in character with his stress on the importance of agape (divine love). One of the most concrete ways of expressing divine love is through concern about another's physical and emotional condition, and the removal of infirmities, hindrances, and the debilitating effects of mental or emotional illness. The healings of Jesus, far from conflicting with his preaching of the kingdom of God, were instead viewed as a direct evidence of it. Jesus stated specifically that his healing was a sign that the kingdom was breaking forth in this world (Matt 12:28). In much the same way Jesus answered the disciples of John the Baptist when they came to inquire if he were the one who was to come or if they should look for another. By quoting the essence of Isaiah 35:5 and 61:1, he pointed to scripture and the messianic hope in these words: "Go and tell John what you hear and see: the blind receive their sight, the lame walk, the lepers are cleansed, the deaf hear, the dead are raised, and the poor have good news brought to them" (Matt 11:4–5). According to this answer, the healing ministry of Jesus was one basic credential and evidence that he was the long-awaited messenger of the kingdom of God. And if Jesus saw himself as the messiah, then he represented God's essential nature, and his healings therefore sprang from the loving nature of God. Sickness and demon possession were considered prime evidences of evil in Jesus' day.[1] By dealing with them as God's agent, Jesus made clear the attitude of God toward sickness.

---

1. Probably the most common ailment Jesus healed was mental illness, generally described in New Testament times as demon possession.

Holistic Happiness

Underlying Jesus' healing attitude was a holistic view of human beings quite unlike most of the ancient world. Jesus had a surprisingly modern theory of human personality. Although implicit, his view of human nature encompassed a highly developed psychological point of view, consistent not only with his ministry but with his ethical outlook, of which his healing ministry was the natural result. As Jesus made clear, most people in their present condition do not deserve or need judgment and punishment, which only drive them further into despair and defeat. People who are sick and in trouble morally need understanding and compassion, not judgment and punishment. Thus, Jesus' attitude toward sin and sickness was in opposition to almost the entire Judaic and Greek culture of his time. At least six of his healings were done on the Sabbath to show his own people how important it was to set aside statutes of external observance when there was an opportunity to help a sick or disable person. And Jesus' treatment of people was not just his own unique approach. It was intended as a general way for people to treat one another, with all sorts of implications beyond his healing ministry.

Recent studies indicate that one person out of every five in the United States over eighteen suffers from at least one recognized psychiatric disorder. Unfortunately, there has been no great advance reducing serious mental sickness, and neurosis can only be conquered by long and costly treatment, which is not always successful. It is important to note that the great majority of the recorded healings of Jesus were either of the mentally ill or of organic disease. It may be easier for us to believe that Jesus could heal mental illness than to accept his physical healings, but those who have experience with mental illness know that this category of disease is more resistant than any other to the advances of modern medicine. Mental illness can be moderated or controlled by drugs, but real healing is rare.

If Jesus had one mission, it was to bring the power and healing of God's creative, loving spirit to bear upon the moral, mental, and physical illnesses of those around him. It was a matter of rescuing people from situations in which they could not help themselves. Jesus' healing actions flowed from his knowledge of our psychological nature as children of God. Significantly, modern medicine has adopted the same nonjudgmental attitude toward healing. The sick person is to be helped and not to be blamed.

More important than knowing who Jesus healed or how he did it is to ask why he did it. The most important reason that Jesus healed was that he cared about people and suffered when they did. Another reason is that he opposed what made people sick. He rebuked the forces that seemed to possess the mentally ill and expressed the same antagonism toward physical illness. Equally important, Jesus healed people to assist their spiritual transformation. He was conscious of the relation between sickness and human frailty and of the human need of wholeness. While he never made human inadequacy or immorality the cause of sickness, he recognized that people who lose their spiritual way, or have none to follow, find themselves exposed to destructive forces that trigger emotional and physical imbalance. If sin be understood as missing the spiritual mark or as turning aside from God's way of wholeness, there is good reason for believing that this can lead to illness. Living in a meaningless world without hope often opens people to fear, hatred, mental distress, meaninglessness, and despair, destructive emotions that embody the cardinal sins. There is good evidence that such emotional disturbances often produce or contribute to a variety of mental and physical illnesses.

If despair and imbalance are the key to sickness, and hope and moderation are key to well-being, as modern psychology indicates, this means we must find ways to welcome the rhythms of life, whether fast or slow, happy or sad, embracing the bad with the good, misfortune and windfall, sickness and health, sorrow and joy. As we seek stability, a good place to begin is with our healing stories and faith journeys. The first account pertains to Jess Dale Costa, my former student and longtime friend, whose input and brilliance provide guidance and inspiration in my series on spirituality and the arts. The second account relates an episode in my current spiritual healing journey.

Jess's Faith Story

My life has been a spiritual journey, though it is hard to discern its periods or stages. What is clear is that my spiritual journey continues daily. Like every journey, there have been landmarks along the way: profound moments of growth, self-doubt, regrowth, revelation, and transformation. Some of those landmarks are in the nature of sudden and mystical enlightenment; others are so subtle that they only unfold over time and through reflection.

I was born a seeker, an artist from the beginning. I sought spirituality as other children seek playgrounds and candy stores. At around seven years of age, I had a fantastic dream of a beautiful spirit beckoning me to come to her in the rose gold clouds. I was in another dimension of reality, a liminal space between the worlds, lost and frightened. When I approached the spirit being, I was only up to her knees, for she was as tall as a tree. However, she radiated a feeling of safety, protection, and peace. She wore radiant rose gold gowns and wrapped me protectively in her flowing capes. I remember this dream in as much detail as I recall something I did just yesterday, and more vividly than my most recent dreams.

Over time, I have come to realize that spiritual moments do not come because I ask for them. God is not a servant who comes when called, to deliver what we expect. Nevertheless, the divine Spirit is always present, providing protection and grace. The concept of grace reminds me that everything is spiritual and that every moment is spiritual, if I only listen for the message and have the patience to wait for it to take shape in my heart. Not everything happens for a reason, but everything is precisely as it should be at any given moment.

By 1995, I was in a bad way. Everything seemed out of control and decades of seeking instant spiritual enlightenment had yielded nothing but a storehouse of theological and mythological ideas. A series of events had taken shape in my life that seemed catastrophic. I was drinking excessively, and was behaving badly, looking for escape in a prolonged drunken stupor. I was a successful lawyer, with my own practice in real estate, municipal law, and estates. I had traveled extensively, had a classical liberal arts education, a law degree, and my own business. Nevertheless, I was drinking incessantly. I became aware that my life was nasty and self-centered, and that I had shut myself from the spiritual growth and experience I had thirsted for since childhood.

A few years earlier, the old willow tree under which I had played and rested had uprooted in a storm. Before the fallen tree could be hauled from our yard, I took some of its wood and carved a small piece into a handle for a walking stick I sometimes carry. Like that tree, I was being uprooted, and nothing would be the same. Sometimes life confronts us with such desolation that all we can do is clutch small pieces of home to remind us of our heritage and to help us move forward into the unknown. I didn't know it at the time, but I was beginning to build, not demolish. My terrain was being cleared for new construction. My father was diagnosed with cancer in 1995, and would die two years later. My mother, who had defied age until now, was beginning to show her age. An only child and still single, I had built my love and life around my parents. They were my only immediate family, but they were old. I felt lost and alone, and saw everything meaningful in my world falling apart.

Holistic Healing

In the late 1980s, the show *Into the Woods* opened on Broadway, and I felt mysteriously drawn to it. Although my interest was primarily artistic and academic, that show would become one of the defining moments in my spiritual life. The metaphor of going into the woods became my own, for the show told my story. Furthermore, it proposed the solution to my dilemma, and its message was exactly what I needed at that point in my life, though I didn't immediately grasp it. The part that took me time to understand comes in the second half of the show, where the characters, who experienced traumatic moments in the woods during the first half, discovered they had to return to the woods.

I was in the woods in 1995, but I was finally finding my way out. Incessant drinking was my solution to an ever-growing set of problems I didn't want to face. One morning in late 1995, I resolved to move forward spiritually. As I could never remember taking my first drink, I cannot recall the exact day I put down my last drink. I only know that one day I realized I wasn't drinking any more, and that I had no desire to do so. Drinking had filled a hole in my soul, but only poorly and temporarily, and at some point drinking stopped working altogether.

That morning in 1995, I confronted my self-doubt and made peace with God and myself. I had no idea then that a more profound spiritual moment lay ahead. That event occurred on March 20, 2017, the first day of spring. As the sun crossed the equator at 6:29 AM, I was sitting outside on a cold snowy morning. Finishing a cup of tea and pondering my life, I felt I was at a crossroads, only the paths weren't clearly defined. As I prayed, I began thinking of favorite readings from Second Corinthians and Revelation 21. Pondering Revelation 21:5, which recounts God's liberating words, "See, I am making all things new," I became aware that this first day of spring was the dawn of my newness. I also realized that God's hopeful message about making all things new isn't once and done, but an ongoing process. Looking back, I realize I was experiencing the newness God had intended for me from the start.

I had formed a clear idea of God in my early teens, for it was then that I came to understand God, who had been a super parent until that point, as a force beyond my grasp, as a mystery called I Am. When I look at critical periods in my life, such as that moment in the winter of 1995 or on the first day of spring in 2017, I realize that my spirituality was taking a turn from intense seeking to comfortable uncertainty. I began making peace with the idea, planted in my mind many years earlier, that all Gods are one God, and that the only truth I need is found in Exodus 3:14, where God's self-revelation is in the affirmation, "I Am." Whereas earlier I believed truth and enlightenment were to be found in pantheistic and dualistic expressions, now I discovered all my previous conceptions of divinity superseded by a view called panentheism, a nondualistic idea that God is the container in which all else is contained. With this perspective in mind, I plunged anew into old theological, mythological, and scriptural studies, with a bias now toward simplification rather than complication.

On the wall of my home, beside the door, hangs a print by my friend Mary Hamilton, entitled "The Way Home." It depicts Merlin, the legendary Welsh mystic and poet, guided back from his own spiritual awakening by a white wolf. According to legend, and in a metaphor oddly reminiscent of Paul's conversion on the road to Damascus, Merlin is temporarily blinded by the power of his own experience. As he wanders, sightless and lost in the wilderness, a white wolf comes to him and guides him home. The way home is to trust the wolf, and the spirit that prompted his awakening.

I had fallen in love with that print a few years before I purchased my home in 1997, always saying that I would have to call Mary and get a print, but never doing so. Hoping the series hadn't sold out, I called her and asked about the print. Thinking for a moment, she believed one might still be in her studio. It was, and I brought it home, grinning from ear to ear and noting that this was a housewarming present for my new house. There is a reason this is the only piece of art in my extensive collection that never rotates. That print doesn't belong to me; rather, it belongs to the space I call home.

Home, I've come to realize, is more than a place. A state of belonging, home is within, not without, the place where all our journeys begin and end. Home is creating a sacred space of our own, and bringing that sacred space within, where we reside.

My Healing Story

Having related my faith story and specific healing episodes in writings such as *Dark Splendor*, *Adventures in Spirituality*, and *In the Potter's Workshop*, here I tell only my most recent healing experience.

Early one morning in 2021, as I was reaching to open my bottom dresser drawer, I felt my lower back lock up. It had been years since my last spinal adjustment, due to the death of my longtime chiropractor and a subsequent diagnosis of osteoporosis. Weakness from osteoporosis eventually led to a compression fracture of one of my thoracic vertebrae, which prevents traditional chiropractic adjustment. Thankfully, I had recovered reasonably well from the compression fracture through therapy, the assistance of a back brace, and over-the-counter pain medication.

The discomfort caused by my subluxation forced me to contact a chiropractor in the area who could work on my back without aggressive spinal manipulation. Able to make an appointment the following day, my first visit involved a thorough evaluation, which led to a twelve-visit program of rehabilitation designed to restore flexibility to my lower back as well as to help reduce or eliminate a kyphosis (an excessive curvature of the back caused, in my case, by osteoporosis) in my upper spine. Midway through the treatment plan, I began noticing significant improvement in my posture.

An active person by nature, I started to take advantage of better posture, taking longer daily walks and increasing my exercise routine to match my improving mental and physical condition. When possible, I exercised in the workout room of my housing clubhouse and in the college gym near my office. On Christmas Day, following a workout, I awoke to soreness in my right knee. I thought about visiting the chiropractor, but I had to wait until after New Year's Day for the office to open, for the practice was closed during the holidays due to relocation. That week I experienced increasing stiffness in my leg and knee, accompanied by progressive loss of mobility and flexibility in my right leg.

Resuming chiropractic treatment in the new year, I discovered that my problem had intensified, and before long it became hard for me to climb steps, stand up without support, or experience normal sleep. By the middle of January, the chiropractor suggested I get an X-ray of my knee, which revealed an arthritic condition and an abundance of fluid in my knee. An appointment with a physician's assistant (PA) confirmed the arthritis and resulted in draining the fluid from my knee, accompanied by a cortisone shot. I felt immediate relief and began regaining flexibility in my knee, and I left the office hoping my problem had been resolved. However, within a day or two the fluid returned, and I was worse off than before. A second visit to the PA led to a another draining of the knee, accompanied by the injection of a solution of hyaluronic acid to lubricate the knee joint and the decision to send a sample of the knee fluid to a lab for diagnosis. A follow-up visit eliminated infection and factors such as gout. However, the fluid had returned and needed to be drained yet again. After additional injections of hyaluronic acid, the PA recommended an MRI of my right knee and set up an appointment with an orthopedic physician.

With the results of my MRI in hand, I visited an orthopedic doctor who had proved invaluable previously in arranging for the diagnosis of my Parsonage-Turner syndrome, a medical condition of unknown cause most likely resulting from autoimmune inflammation. On this occasion, however, the doctor was puzzled as to the cause of the fluid buildup and retention in my knee. While the MRI revealed a slight tear in the lateral meniscus and some fraying of the medial meniscus, it appeared that such damage was not recent, and likely not the reason for the fluid buildup. Draining the knee once again, he decided to send the fluid for additional testing and arranged a visit with an orthopedic surgeon a week later.

The eight-day wait seemed endless. The pain medication and anti-inflammatory drugs I was taking were ineffective, and sleeping had become practically impossible, for I was unable to find a position on the bed that did not aggravate my leg. By the time I visited the surgeon, I was desperate, feeling that I needed a decisive solution regarding my pain and discomfort. My visit resulted in further indecision, for like the diagnosis of the first physician, the surgeon was not convinced that the fluid buildup was caused by the minor damage in my knee. He told me of a previous patient whose condition had been similar to mine, but who had experienced no relief from surgery. Knowing that the fluid was having a degenerative effect on my knee, he drained the fluid yet again, agreeing to see me a week later.

Suspecting an autoimmune condition, he prescribed a powerful steroid, a six-day Medrol pack for immune system disorder, noting that surgery remained an option. Needing quick relief, I began taking the Medrol medication immediately. The results were dramatic; the pain and inflammation in my knee subsided overnight, and I was finally able to sleep for more than an hour at a time.

As I awaited the follow-up appointment with the surgeon, I embraced an idea I had known only cognitively, that God speaks clearly and persuasively through pain. As C. S. Lewis famously noted, "pain insists upon being attended to. God whispers to us in our pleasure, speaks in our conscience, but shouts in our pain. Pain is God's megaphone, to rouse a deaf world."[2] Paradoxically, natural pain is an expression of divine love, and even when caused by inhumane violence or abuse, it can serve as a beacon lighting our way home.

As I consulted with my wife Susan, a Gestalt Pastoral Care minister who had survived a cancer operation, including chemotherapy and radiation

---

2. Lewis, *Problem of Pain*, 93.

Holistic Healing

treatment, through meditation and contemplation, I soon realized that healing had to come from within. "Your body produced and sent the fluid to your knee for a reason yet unknown," Susan told me, "and you might try encouraging it to reverse itself. Start practicing meditation at least twice daily, accessing healing through your shadow side."[3] Knowing me to be impatient and competitive and to take a hands-on approach to life, she recommended that I set aside my "take-charge" style by practicing "letting go."

"Instead of trying to control your situation," she seemed to be saying, "allow the Divine Healer to work from within." As doctors and medical science know, the body heals itself. Science provides the tools for proper diagnosis, but spirituality provides the results. As a minister who values science, Susan knows that contemplation allows practitioners to access their theta brain waves, associated with light sleep but also found in deeply relaxed states of mind sometimes described as daydreaming or "autopilot," as well as in hypnosis and activities such as visualization and visioning. Experts believe that theta waves are important for neurological activities such as processing information and making memories, but, like other brain waves, they also play important roles in health and wellness.

Though Susan's approach conflicted with my "Type A" personality, the results of taking her suggestions were impressive, As she was aware, it was time for me take the advice of a valued scriptural passage: "Trust in the Lord with all your heart, and do not rely on your own insight. In all your ways acknowledge him, and he will make straight your paths" (Prov 3:5–6).

The follow-up visit with my surgeon proved a pleasant surprise, for he could see the positive results. When I told him my painful symptoms were subsiding he replied, "I can tell the results simply by looking at your face." When I asked him to inspect my knee, he responded, "I don't have to. The improvement is obvious! A systemic approach was needed, and I'm glad you are getting better." I left with a script for a rheumatologist, an indication of the doctor's desire for comprehensive treatment.

The following morning was "the first day of the rest of my life." I needed to stop relying on medication and begin trusting my God-given resourcefulness. In addition to my regular morning exercise routine and without overdoing it, I felt it was time to start rehabbing my right leg by incorporating it more fully and aggressively in my workouts. Today was

---

3. The shadow self, something everyone possesses, represents the least developed part of one's personality. The shadow uses relatively childish and primitive forms of judgment and perception, often as an escape from the conscious personality and in defiance of conscious standards.

the day I would rise from a sitting position with minimal support and begin walking boldly up steps. Guided by the holistic wisdom of "spirit over mind, and mind over body," I told my body and brain that it was time to stop living fearfully and to begin walking confidently once again. Faith is essential to wellness, and I needed to trust God by trusting my healing.

While confidence is a good quality, overconfidence is not. After making significant physical progress, I began to question the wisdom of further medical intervention. However, the day before my appointment with the rheumatologist, my hopes were dashed and my progress was nullified by an early morning fainting spell that resulted in a hard fall on the bathroom floor. Upon recovery, I could hardly move. Thankfully, I had no broken bones, but the fall caused a bad sprain in my right ankle, soreness in my right knee, pain across my lower back, and a lump on my forehead.

Seeing the nasty swelling around my ankle, my wife filled a small tub with ice water and that began a new start to my healing process. My visit with the rheumatologist resulted in the ordering of numerous follow-up tests, and a visit to my chiropractor included his warning that the pain and distress would likely increase before I got better. That was confirmed when I received the results of my bloodwork, which showed that I had tested positive for Lyme disease. Suddenly things began to make sense; my recovery proved to be long and arduous, and pain would continue its mentoring process for I still had much to learn.

My journey eventually led me to Erika Shinya, a certified core synchronism practitioner and a graduate of New Mexico School of Natural Therapeutics, who uses touch in working with the body when it experiences pain and discomfort and is in need of balance. Utilizing the energy in cerebrospinal fluid, she is able to utilize nature and a person's essential life force to balance his or her body holistically. After two sessions I began experiencing an increase in flexibility, strength, and vitality, sensing natural shifts in my body's entire skeletal structure to correct asynchronous motion that caused pain and discomfort. I began feeling more relaxed and at peace while experiencing renewed energy, vitality, greater flexibility, and optimal functioning. I still couldn't run a marathon, but I was able to take longer walks, stand up effortlessly, breathe and sleep better, and gradually able to walk up steps more naturally.

As it turns out, healing stories can be deeply spiritual, and faith stories profoundly healing. In my case, I had much to learn spiritually, and I am convinced that further physical healing will include additional spiritual growth, including attaining the discernment that comes when I learn to listen for and obey promptings of the divine Spirit speaking through my circumstances.

As Jess's faith story and my healing account indicate, when human beings are in need of healing, physically, emotionally, and spiritually, they should ask God, not because God dwells in heaven and is able to utilize supernatural resources, but because God is here with us now. In other words, God is both transcendent and immanent, but immanence is the key to God's transcendence. Because God made nature, God is in nature and, at least in some essential way, *is* nature. Acknowledging God's presence with us is part of the meaning of the doctrine of the incarnation. As incarnation indicates, Jesus is Emmanuel (God with us). However, God has always been with us, and not simply for a few decades in the first century. Jesus may be the best human representation of God's character on earth, but he is not the only exemplar of God on earth. God was in nature from the beginning, and never left. God has been with us and in us all along.

Healing, like all change and transformation in our lives, requires faith in the laws and the processes of nature. As Jesus taught, God's kingdom is within us, and learning to live in this kingdom means learning to tap into the power and light of God within. However, as we have seen, God works in and through the circumstances of our lives, because healing essentially follows laws and processes in nature. What this means is that both physical wellness and spiritual wholeness are not supernatural but rather natural phenomena. The spiritual principle to remember here is this: God does not minister *to* us, but rather *through* us. Like all spiritual growth and transformation, healing is a cooperative venture. God initiates the healing process, but uses nature to accomplish the results. As soon as we realize that God does this *through* us (not *for* us), healing becomes as simple as breathing and as inevitable as sunrise.

God is both within us and without us, both within nature and beyond nature. God is the source of all life and all reality. Despite such transcendence, God also indwells each individual human self. However, just as an electric appliance cannot work unless it is prepared to receive electricity, so the infinite and eternal power of God cannot help us unless we are prepared to receive that power within ourselves.

God is not a capricious or impulsive sovereign who breaks natural laws at will. When we say that God is omnipotent, we understand that God made a world that runs by law, and furthermore, that God does not capriciously break natural laws. In terms of personal healing and transformation, we can only access the amount of God that we are prepared to receive. Please pause and think about this principle for a moment, for it is central to healing. If there is some sin in our lives, some obstruction blocking God's healing power, spiritual electricity cannot flow and healing is impeded. What this means in practical terms is that God wills our healing, but is often prevented from doing so by some obstruction in us. Of course, God may delay or prevent healing for reasons unknown to us.

Just as we don't correctly understand all the laws of nature, so we don't yet understand how God heals. Some day we will understand the scientific principles that underlie the miracle-working power of God, and we will accept God's intervention as simply and naturally as we understand radios, televisions, and computers. God does nothing except by natural law. However, God has provided enough power within those laws to do anything that is in accordance with divine will. It is our task to work within God's will, and to seek the simplicity and beauty of the laws that release God's power.

Let us be clear: no human being has the power to heal physically, emotionally, or spiritually. All spiritual wholeness and wellness come from God, If the principles of divine healing can be reduced to three, the first step is to contact God's power. The second step is to turn that power on, and the third step is to affirm that this power is flowing through us and to accept it by faith. However, no matter how much we ask God for something, it becomes ours only as we accept it and give thanks for it. Of course, not all healing is instantaneous.

If we understand healing and spiritual growth, not as the breaking of natural laws but as God using them for divine purpose, then the world is full of miracles. The job of spirituality is to prepare us to receive God's transformative spiritual energy. As we progress spiritually, so we grow in wisdom, vitality, and wholeness.

Questions for Discussion and Reflection

In addition to the questions listed at the end of the preface, answer the following questions, writing your answers in a journal. If you are in a group study, be prepared to share your answers with those in the group.

1. In your estimation, should mainline Protestant denominations emphasize spiritual healing as part of their ministry or continue to focus

Holistic Healing

on traditional worship and issues such as fellowship, evangelism, counseling, justice, and ecumenism? Explain your answer.

2. If physical and mental healing were central to Jesus' ministry, why have most Christian churches discontinued this emphasis or practice?
3. If, as Jesus made clear, people who are sick and in trouble morally need compassion and understanding rather than judgment or condemnation, explain why these principles have been reversed by institutional Christianity.
4. In your own words, explain your understanding of the relationship between spirituality and wellness, including mental and physical health and well-being.
5. After reading Jess's faith story, what did you learn about the role of spirituality in holistic living?
6. After reding the author's healing story, what did you learn about the role of spirituality in holistic healing?
7. Explain the meaning of the author's statement, "immanence is the key to God's transcendence"?
8. Explain the meaning of the author's statement, "God does not minister *to* us, but rather *through* us."
9. Explain and assess the meaning of the author's statement, "we can only access the amount of God that we are prepared to receive."
10. Assess the validity of the author's statement that "God wills our healing but is often prevented from doing so by some (sin or) obstruction in us."
11. Assess the meaning of the author's statement that "God does nothing except by natural law."

4

Holistic Theology

THEOLOGY IS "TALK ABOUT God." However, because theology is about God, it is also about cosmology and anthropology, for how we see God influences, even determines, how we see the world around us and within us. It is important that we understand God correctly, because there is an absolute connection between our beliefs about the nature of the cosmos (if it was created by God and whether it was created totally good at the point of its creation) and how we relate to ourselves and to others. This is why good theology, healthy psychology, and holistic spirituality can make a major difference in our self-image and in how we live with others.

In his 1976 book, *Forgotten Truth*, the renowned scholar of comparative religions, Huston Smith, delves into the "primordial tradition," the common, fundamental experience of humankind, as found in the core teachings of the world's religions, identifying therein a cosmology based on the idea of an ontological gradation of reality.

According to Smith, the "primordial tradition" is perhaps best distinguished by its recognition of the many-layered nature of both reality and the self. Smith narrows these layers to four: reality is composed of the terrestrial, intermediate, celestial, and infinite levels, while the self is composed of the body, mind, soul, and spirit.

These tiers correlate in such a way that higher levels of reality correspond to deeper levels of the self:

- The terrestrial tier (also called the material, physical, sensible, corporeal, and phenomenal) corresponds to the body.

- The intermediate tier (also called the subtle, psychic, astral, or demonic realm) corresponds to the mind.
- The celestial tier (this realm views God as personal; here one speaks of God's attributes and personality) corresponds to the soul.
- The Infinite tier (this realm views God as transpersonal; this level is best spoken of through analogy, in negative terms, or through paradox) corresponds to the spirit.

Smith's cosmological image shows the earth, symbolic of the terrestrial sphere, enveloped by the intermediate sphere, which in turn is enclosed by the celestial, the three concentric spheres together superimposed on a background that represents the Infinite. "Considered in itself, each sphere appears as a complete and homogeneous whole, while from the perspective of the area that encloses and permeates it, it is but a content. Thus the terrestrial world knows not the intermediate world, or the latter the celestial, though each world is known and dominated by the one that exceeds and enfolds it."[1] With each higher level, different laws apply, together with a different way of experiencing reality. The highest and deepest tiers, Infinite and spirit, are, according to Smith, without limitation; while the Infinite is unbounded externally, the human spirit is unbounded internally. These two levels, therefore, are in fact the same.

As one moves down the tiers of reality and out the tiers of selfhood, one encounters increasing levels of differentiation and/or materialization. In the primordial tradition, the possibility exists that one of the higher metaphysical levels can "break through" into one of the lower levels, in so doing overriding the laws of that lower level. While religion explores all four levels holistically, the laws of science are limited in their application primarily to the physical (terrestrial) level.

According to Smith, the human self consists of four levels, configured concentrically as body, mind, soul, and spirit. Whereas Smith places the body in the innermost circle, as the most accessible aspect, with the other levels expanding concentrically outward to the spirit, humanity's most expansive element, I think of the body as the outermost level, the container for the inner levels of selfhood. Next is the mind, the seat of consciousness, conceived as distinct from the brain, which is a part of the body. This distinction is based on the perspective of neurophysiologists such as Wilder Penfield, who argue for the uniqueness of the mind, which "seems to act

---

1. Smith, *Forgotten Truth*, 61.

independently of the brain in the same sense that a programmer acts independently of his computer."[2] According to Smith, there is no convincing materialistic explanation of mind, for mind cannot be measured quantitatively. Furthermore, mind plays by different rules, conforming to laws that differ in kind from those that matter exemplifies.

The third level of selfhood is the soul (called by ancients *psyche, anima, atman, nephesh,* or *nafs*), the final locus of our individuality, its source and yet superior. The soul is closer to our essence than is the mind, with which we usually identify; its tropism is toward being and its increase.[3] While the soul is finite, it is the only possible bridge to spirit, the fourth level of selfhood. If soul is the element in humans that relates to God, spirit is the element that is identical with God, not with God's personal mode but with God's mode that is infinite. Mystics and theologians speak of identity at this level because "on this final stratum the subject-object dichotomy is transcended."[4] While Spirit is infinite, humans remain finite because they are not spirit only. Our specifically human overlay—body, mind, and soul—veils the Spirit within us.

The key point in Smith's model is the realization that as far as selfhood is concerned, one cannot maintain harmony, equilibrium, and flow by jumping across levels. Each level builds consecutively and concentrically on the preceding. In other words, the bridge to consciousness is the body. To understand the mind, one must be fully grounded in one's physicality. The link to soul is mind, and the link to spirit is soul. Each level must be explored deeply and authentically before it can serve as conduit to the next. To acquire meaning and understanding, one cannot jump from body to soul or from mind to spirit. For Smith, the final link, the door that leads from soul to spirit, is love: love of "Being-as-a whole or of the God who is its Lord. For Spirit to permeate the self's entirety, the components of the self must be aligned: body in temperance, mind in understanding, and soul in love."[5]

As I note frequently in my writings, spirituality is the journey of life "from God, to God, and with God." As a result, it is also a journey toward the self. In other words, the process of coming to know or to experience God is also the process of knowing oneself.

---

2. Smith, *Forgotten Truth*, 64.
3. Smith, *Forgotten Truth*, 76.
4. Smith, *Forgotten Truth*, 87.
5. Smith, *Forgotten Truth*, 92.

Holistic Theology

Viewed globally and interreligiously, the central defining characteristic of spirituality is an individual's connection to a greater whole. At its heart, spirituality involves an emotional experience of awe and reverence, an experience natural to most of our human ancestors. They had a wonderful idea of God because they lived in an awesome world. They wondered at the magnificence of whatever it was that brought the world into being. This led to a sense of adoration. This adoration, this gratitude, we call religion. Building on this foundation, Western spirituality contributed an understanding of a sovereign Creator God who initiates, maintains, and unifies reality in a loving and gracious manner.

In modern times, however, the outer world has taken priority, and as a result, our inner spiritual world is drying up. The task of spirituality is to help us regain our sense of awe and reverence, beginning with a profound commitment to God, but an equal commitment to nature, to the whole of humanity, and to every living creature. If we do not love what is visible around us, how can we love God, whom we cannot see? (1 John 4:19-20).

How we conceive God determines how we experience God. Is God personal? The Christian tradition, as most religions, views God thus, with personal characteristics. Supernatural theism is unambiguously anthropomorphic. The natural language of meditation, devotion, and corporate worship is personal; we use this language regularly in our private devotional life and when we worship in church. There is nothing wrong with personifying God and addressing God as if God were a person.

Problems arise, however, when we literalize these personifications, as though "the right hand of God" means that God really has hands, and when God is said to speak, that God must have a larynx. Some years ago, a group of Baptists left the Texas Baptist Convention because they believed that God is male rather than female or sexless. Did they believe, I wonder, that God has male sex organs? If so, does God have to shave? Of course, such questions seem trivial, but they are not unimportant.

Perhaps we can ease some of the difficulty by a softer literalization of personal language for God, namely, by affirming that God is personlike. This means that God is separate from the universe, a living being separate from other beings and yet somewhat like us, though to a superlative degree. Nevertheless, literalizing these personifications leads to supernatural theism and the problems associated with it, such as the apparent contradiction between God's omnipotence, justice, and omnibenevolence. Human experience of God suggests that God cannot simultaneously be all-powerful, all-good, and all-loving, else there would be less injustice and tragedy in this world and more goodness and morality. Likewise, the biblical view of God can be an impediment to belief, for this God seems to display unattractive and even immoral behavior, displayed through qualities such as destructive anger, jealousy, and biased treatment of human beings. This God is depicted as choosing people selectively, fighting wars, defeating enemies, sending storms, plagues, and even death. Yet this God also heals the sick, spares the dying, and rewards goodness. Even normal human judgment condemns such behavior as inconsistent and immoral. In his publication *The Sins of Scripture*, Bishop Spong examines biblical moral principles attributed to the will of God and concludes that those who wish to base their morality literally on the Bible have either not read it or not understood it.

In 1986 John F. Haught, one of our most insightful Christian scholars, wrote a short work titled *What is God? How to Think About the Divine*. Writing for skeptical individuals who question whether talk about God is obsolete, Haught proposed that we alter the way we think about God; instead of using personal terms to describe God—asking "who" God is—he suggests that we focus instead on "what" God is, focusing on the transpersonal or superpersonal aspect to God found in many religious traditions, aspects of deity that cannot be adequately represented in personalistic imagery. This approach is helpful ontologically as well as intellectually.

Ontologically, an examination of the transpersonal dimension of God's nature, that side of God's being that cannot be adequately represented in personalistic terms, may help us to make some sense of the "scandal" of the divine hiddenness. Intellectually, thinkers ask questions like "What is nature?" "What is history?" "What is the universe?" Those are the questions of inquiry, so in that intellectual environment it seems appropriate to ask also "What is God?" Haught's project isn't to demonstrate the existence of God, but rather to help us think about God, thereby arguing that a case can be made for taking seriously the possibility that God is.

The suspicion of God's existence that one finds in the writings of Nietzsche, Marx, and Freud is shared by many intellectuals today. Noting a serious question today among scientific thinkers, philosophers, and many other intelligent people as to whether the word "God" actually refers to any genuinely real dimension of our experience, Haught claims that talk about "God" may be little more that whistling in the dark or a cover-up for human weakness. Given the trite and personalistic ways the idea of God has been employed by many "religious" people, such suspicion is often justified. But the word "God" can mean much more than this.

Haught contends that the idea of God was not a theoretical construct invented by theologians but came to human consciousness spontaneously as the product of religious experience, as a response to the sense of the "sacred," a phenomenon Rudolf Otto termed the *mysterium tremendum et fascinans*. Originally described in the language of symbol and myth, this experience "was acted out in ritual and other kinds of human activity long before it became a topic of philosophical or theological discussion."[6] Modern reflection on God should utilize similar symbolic categories, ones that can be identifiable in the experience of all human beings and not simply "religious" people.

Building on the contributions of depth psychology, process theology, and the insights of important twentieth-century religious thinkers such as Alfred North Whitehead, Paul Tillich, Paul Ricoeur, Bernard Lonergan, and Karl Rahner, Haught identifies five experiential human notions as the locus for conceptualizing deity: depth, future, freedom, beauty, and truth. While there is something undeniably "real" about each of these aspects of conscious existence, there is something elusive about them as well. Like our idea of God, such experiences are either bio-psychological phenomena that refer to nothing beyond themselves, or they point beyond themselves to a Source that grounds them—which Source is a God candidate.

Utilizing these five categories enables Haught to emphasize what he calls the "neuter" rather than the masculine and feminine images ordinarily evoked by religious symbolism, the "whatness" rather than the "whoness" of God. Considered the leading figure in the development of twentieth-century hermeneutics, German philosopher Hans-Georg Gadamer relates how his teacher, Martin Heidegger, once observed: "Who is God? That is perhaps beyond the possibilities of our asking. But what is God? That we should ask."[7] And Gadamer thinks that we should pay more attention to neuter expressions such as "the divine" or "the sacred," terms that occurs frequently in poetry: "I think the neuter is one of the most mysterious things in human language . . . To use the neuter—for example, 'the beautiful'—expresses something of ungraspable presence. It is no longer 'this' or 'that,' male or female, here or there; it is filling empty space . . . The neuter represents in a way the plenitude of presence, the omnipresence of something.

---

6. Haught, *What is God?*, 2–3.
7. Cited in Haught, *What is God?*, 8.

Hence the divine is indeed an expression for such omnipresence."[8] Thus, while inadequate in itself, the neuter in our thinking of God is a helpful corrective to a one-sided personalistic understanding.

There are clearly problems associated with personalistic and impersonalistic personifications of God, for as theologians indicate, God is Subject and not object, and therefore the best way to conceive God is through paradox and mystery. Hence, it is appropriate to affirm God as simultaneously being and nonbeing, existent and nonexistent, and therefore equally personal and impersonal, gendered and nongendered, neuter and androgynous, Whatever God is ultimately like, whether personal, impersonal, or transpersonal (that is, more than personal), there are at least three dimensions of meaning to personal language of God that we need to retain:

- God's relationship to us is personal. It is doubtful that humans could worship something that does not have at least the status of personality.
- God has more the quality of "presence" than of nonpersonal "energy" or "force." To use language coined by the Jewish philosopher Martin Buber, God has the quality of a "Thou" rather than that of an "It," hence more the quality of a person than of an impersonal "source."
- God communicates with us, not necessarily audibly or by divine dictation, but God "speaks," sometimes through visions and dreams but also through "prodding" or "hunches." Vehicles for these can include other people, devotional practices, the scriptures of one's religious tradition, and daily circumstances.

As contemporary author Frederick Buechner advises, "Listen to your life. Listen to what happens to you because it is through what happens to you that God speaks." Paula D'Arcy states this truth more bluntly: "God comes to you disguised as your life."

Does God exist? Is there a deity somewhere within or beyond the known universe? The only true answer is nobody knows for sure. No ordinary human being, whether in the past or in the present, has been able to offer conclusive evidence either for the existence or the nonexistence of a deity, however defined, envisioned, or experienced. With regard to the existence or nonexistence of God, all of us are agnostic. Some of us lean toward theism, others toward atheism, but beyond one cannot go.

---

8. Cited in Haught, *What is God?*, 8.

Holistic Theology

As the Christian scriptures make clear, all God language and God experience is faith based. Whatever one believes or disbelieves, the supportive argumentation is merely an extension of that person's faith orientation, presuppositional base, or intuitive worldview. As we learn from modern philosophy, all so-called proofs for the existence or nonexistence of God are but footnotes to one's assumptive stance. Meaningful human discourse or reflection on the existence or nonexistence of God requires acknowledgement of assumptive premises and starting points.

The next concern when speaking about of God involves identifying the specific understanding or view of God being affirmed or denied. Quite frequently thoughtful theists and atheists find themselves agreeing on caricatures or stereotypes of God they mutually reject, such as God's supposed omnipotence and omnibenevolence, contradictory concepts at best. Unless one espouses biblical inerrancy or doctrinal infallibility, all God-talk is figurative in nature and all Christian theology provisional. If you find a statement about God helpful or relevant, adopt it with caution and examine it carefully. Conversely, if you find a statement about God problematic or irrelevant, approach it with an open and inquisitive mind before you modify or reject it.

Viewing God as Father, Son, and Holy Spirit

In Christian usage, the word "God" is a both verb and a noun. Because God is active and dynamic, God is relational. As "Father, Son, and Holy Spirit," God is three "relations," understood as formlessness (Father), as form (Son), and as the divine energy binding Father and Son (Holy Spirit). At its heart, spirituality, traditionally defined by Christians as "life in the Spirit," envisions the journey of life from a distinct perspective. In my estimation, the Christian notion of God as Trinity is foundational to spirituality, for this understanding views God as both singular and plural, as "being" yet also as "nonbeing," simultaneously personal, impersonal, and transpersonal.

Using the analogy of love, the medieval theologian Augustine of Hippo viewed the Father as Lover or subject of divine love, the Son as Beloved or object of divine love, and the Spirit as the bond of love between Father and Son, as the divine energy binding God and all reality. Defining theology (God) and spirituality (Spirit) as Relationship moves us away from vague abstraction and opens conversation with the world of science, for it helps us to understand the cohesive mystery permeating all reality, from atoms, to ecosystems, to galaxies. If the nature of God is the nature of everything, then everything in the universe is in relationship and nothing stands alone.

Children are taught certain things about the nature of God at an early age. Many of these teachings prove to be immensely helpful and provide a sound basis for later development, but many are also confusing and lead to distortion. For example, some parents use a God image to help maintain discipline and control. They portray God as a stern judge, a severe taskmaster who keeps an ongoing tally of the child's deeds and misdeeds. Other parents, perhaps in an attempt to prevent such harshness, present God as Love, thereby avoiding all anthropomorphism. For small children, this image may be too abstract to integrate in a meaningful way. While it preserves the mystery of God, it does not give children someone personal to whom they can pray or with whom to relate. The image of God as "Father," commonly used, is inevitably influenced by the child's human father, and thereby can restrict children's experiences in meditation, worship, and prayer.

Regardless of what images are presented by parents, most children develop a sense of God as being active in their lives. They see God as a person or force that influences their daily activities, bringing good things or abandoning them to bad things. In either case, they relate to God through appeasement, much as adults do when they are frightened or despairing.

Within each of us is a deep desire for intimacy with God, with our truest self, and with all of creation. Because life is difficult, and we are wired for survival, we develop coping mechanisms that separate us from each other and from God. At some point it becomes clear that images of God are not God. As people mature and grow spiritually, some images of God die and are replaced by others, while some images remain deep within, unchanging yet affecting human experience.

Jesus is one of the clearest images of God's love. His teaching and example model for us what it means to be both human and divine—at the same time. He dismantles our preconceived ideas about who and where God is and is not. Jesus made room for the new by letting go of the old. John the Baptist described Jesus as a "winnowing fork" that separates the grain from the chaff (see Matt 3:12). If we don't winnow, we spend a lot of time protecting the "chaff" or non-essentials. Jesus did not let the old get in the way of the new, but rather revealed what the old was saying all along. Jesus conserved what was worth conserving and prevented non-essentials from getting in the way. While honoring and emphasizing the core elements of his tradition, he ignored and even undercut most non-essential religious rules and norms. This is invariably the character of any reformer, to follow the Spirit's leading.

When we think of Jesus, I suggest we think of the historical human being who represents for Christians the ideal universal person, the embodiment of the highest and best in us all. Had Jesus no other legacy, he would be remembered as one of the world's master teachers. Jesus, however, did not come on the scene to conform to anyone's preconceived expectation about sages, or for that matter, about prophets or messiahs. His subject, essentially, was threefold: he made known something about God, something about humankind, and something about their interrelationship.

Apart from the tradition of Judaism, however, the life or teaching of Jesus would have been incomprehensible. In Jesus' day there was a vast human quest for God, wrapped up in piety and legalism (Judaism), and in idolatry and superstition (Gentiles). The Jews were monotheists and had a central temple in Jerusalem, dedicated to sacrifice and rituals. Much of their worship was motivated by duty and regulated by tradition. However, no code of laws can deal with the variety of human beings. While Jesus affirmed the value of Jewish law in many of his actions and teachings, he regularly pointed beyond the law. According to Jesus, each of us has individual value and our own unique journey to God.

Whatever more he is—or was—Jesus must be one of us. If Jesus is to be our Person, our Man, he must be a human being in every sense of the word. This is what we find in the New Testament. The early Christians began with a view of Christ that was uncomplicated and relatable. They certainly did not see Jesus to be of *merely* human significance, since he embodied what God was doing in their midst. But their earliest memory was fashioned into a simplistic Christology, perhaps the earliest, of "a man," Jesus of Nazareth, singled out by God, crucified and raised from the dead, as Peter's speech on the day of Pentecost recalls (Acts 2:22–24). "This Jesus God raised up, and of that all of us are witnesses. Being therefore exalted at the right hand of God, and having received from the Father the promise of the Holy Spirit, he has poured out this that you both see and hear" (Acts 2:32–33).

Who, then, was Jesus, and what, from the historical records, can we infer about him? Despite belonging to the Jewish peasant class, he was minimally literate, in that he undoubtedly went to school in the synagogue in Nazareth, where the emphasis would have been on reading and writing, with the Torah as the primary text. He became a woodworker, which, in terms of social standing, placed him at the lower end of the peasant class, more marginalized than a peasant who still owned a small piece of land.

At some point in his life Jesus embarked upon a religious quest. He probably underwent what William James calls a "conversion experience," not, of course, from paganism to Judaism, for he grew up Jewish. Conversion, as James defines it, need not infer a change from one religion to another, or from being nonreligious to being religious. It can refer to a process of internal transformation, whether sudden or gradual, which led him to undertake his ministry. Influenced by a fiery preacher known as John the Baptist, in his late twenties or around the age of thirty he embarked on his career. Mark dates the beginning of Jesus' ministry to John's arrest, which suggests that, with his mentor in prison, Jesus stepped in to carry on.

What was the adult Jesus like, and what did he come to understand about himself and his mission? All understandings of Christianity rely ultimately on two assessments: Jesus' self-understanding and the early church's conceptualizing of that self-understanding. Let us start with the obvious: Jesus was deeply Jewish. Not only was he Jewish by birth and socialization, but he remained a Jew all of his life. His scripture was the Jewish Bible. He did not intend to establish a new religion, but saw himself as having a mission within Judaism. He spoke as a Jew to other Jews. His early followers were Jewish.

Jesus became a gifted teacher. His verbal gifts were remarkable. His language was most often metaphorical, poetic, and imaginative, filled with memorable short sayings and compelling short stories we call parables. He was clearly exceptionally intelligent. Like the classical prophets of ancient Israel, he performed symbolic actions. On one occasion he staged a demonstration in the temple, overturning the tables of the money changers and driving out the sellers of sacrificial animals. There was a radical social and political edge to his message and activity, as he challenged the social order of his day and indicted the elites who dominated it. He must have been remarkably courageous, willing to continue what he was doing even when in lethal danger. He was a remarkable healer: more healing stories are told about him than about anybody else in the Jewish tradition. He attracted a following, which means he was quite compelling. He also attracted enemies, especially among the rich and powerful. Unlike the founders of the world's other major religious traditions, his public ministry was brief, lasting at most three or four years. Living only into his early thirties, he was then crucified on charges of sedition. At his crucifixion the Romans placed an inscription on his cross that read, "Jesus of Nazareth, King of the Jews," thereby issuing a warning to his followers that Roman rule would not tolerate insurrection.

Holistic Theology

In the sixty or seventy years after Jesus' death, when the Easter traditions found in the New Testament took shape, Jewish Christian communities searched the Hebrew scriptures, finding a large number of metaphors or images that related to Jesus and his significance, images such as servant of God, lamb of God, light of the world, bread of life, Lord, door, vine, shepherd, messiah, savior, great high priest, sacrifice, Son of God, Son of Man, Wisdom of God, and Word of God. Over time, these metaphors became the subject of intellectual reflection and conceptualization. Some, ultimately, became doctrine. This process produced the post-Easter Jesus—the "Christ of faith"—of Christian tradition.

As a result of reading the New Testament, filtered through the creeds of later Christendom, Christians have arrived at an understanding of Jesus that is quite different from the sketch presented above. That understanding might be summarized under the phrase "Christian messiah," an exalted status that includes such titles of Jesus as "Son of God," "Word of God," "Wisdom of God," "Lamb of God," "Light of the World," "Bread of Life," "Alpha and Omega," and "firstborn of all creation." These may not convey what Jesus of Nazareth thought or taught about himself, but they came to summarize what New Testament Christians believed Jesus to be.

While Jesus may be the best human representation of God we have, "God in the flesh," "one with God" if you will, he was not fully God, but rather a sacramental "thin place," a person fully transparent to the divine. In *The Meaning of Jesus*, a book coauthored with conservative theologian N. T. Wright, college professor Marcus Borg tells the story of a bright Muslim engineering student who enrolled in his introductory level course on the Bible. One day, after witnessing the first few weeks of his liberal professor's interaction with some of his articulate conservative students, the engineering student came to Dr. Borg and said, "I think I understand what's going on here. You're saying the Bible is like a lens through which we see God, and they're saying that it's important to believe in the lens." Borg agreed with his student's assessment, and finding this to be a teaching moment, used the lens analogy to make two further points. First, if the Bible is a lens through which we see God, it should not be the object of our belief, for Christianity is not primarily about believing in a lens, but about entering a deepening relationship to that which we see through the lens. Hence, Christianity is not about believing in the Bible or the gospels or in teachings about Jesus, but about "a relationship to the One we see through the lens of the Christian tradition as a whole."[9] According to Borg, Jesus is a lens, the decisive lens through which we see God and what a life full of God is like. He is the incarnation of the word, wisdom, compassion, and passion of God. If the Christian life is essentially a relationship with God, then Jesus is also the primary lens through which we see what a life filled with God's Spirit looks like, for Jesus lived a life centered in the Spirit.

While it is clear biblically, historically, and theologically that Jesus was physically male, it is not clear that he was psychologically, emotionally, and spiritually male, certainly by current standards. In fact, as a straightforward reading of the gospels indicates, the historical Jesus is best understood as having been androgynous, or, in current parlance, *spiritually* non-binary, for he displayed archetypal male and female spirituality fully and equally. When Swiss psychiatrist Carl Jung spoke of Jesus as "the Archetype of the Self," he meant that the qualities and priorities Jesus manifested in his life and ministry served as a template for full and authentic human life, fully integrating male and female spirituality.

According to the Eastern yin-yang model of the self and of reality, most things are on a continuum between yin and yang. For instance, all males have some yin, and all females some yang. The ideal male, for example, might be 80 percent yang and 20 percent yin. Likewise, the ideal female might be 80 percent yin and 20 percent yang. When yin and yang work together in harmony, life is as it should be. The brilliant word, nonduality, used by many cultural and religious traditions, celebrates difference and affirms diversity. It simply refuses to see this diversity as anything other than the greater unity of a singular Reality. There is no question that Paul is thinking along nondual lines when he writes in Galatians 3:28, "There is no longer Jew or Greek, there is no longer slave or free, there is no longer male and female; for all of you are one in Christ Jesus." Likewise, when Jesus answers Philip's request to "Show us the Father" (14:8), Jesus' answer is emphatic: "Whoever has seen me has seen the Father" (14:9). While the union between Jesus and the Father has been described as mystical, moral, or metaphysical, these are misleading, for none capture John's essential understanding of agency. The point is not that Jesus is the Father, but that he is the expression of the very mind and character of God.

According to Christian teaching, it is not only through Jesus but also through the Holy Spirit that we touch God not as a concept but as a living reality. According to John's gospel, God's Holy Spirit functions as a Paraclete

---

9. Borg and Wright, *Meaning of Jesus*, 239–40.

(advocate, intercessor, helper, comforter). Paraclete is not simply another name for the Spirit, but is a particular way of describing the functions of the Spirit, functions held in common with Jesus. What the Paraclete does is not new, but is a continuation of the work of Jesus. This can be seen clearly in the description of the Paraclete as the "spirit of truth" (14:7). As the Spirit of truth, the Paraclete shares in the work of Jesus, because Jesus is the truth (14:6). The work of the Paraclete is thus to keep the truth of Jesus present in the world after Jesus' departure (16:7–11). As we read in John's gospel and in the book of Acts, the Spirit's role has much to do with the essential condition and function of disciples after Jesus' lifetime.

When Jesus says that the Father will give "another" Paraclete (John 14:6), John evidently intends for readers to understand Jesus as having been a Paraclete also. The Spirit's role as Paraclete is to continue doing what Jesus began. The language of agency is particularly appropriate here: as Jesus was the Father's agent, so the Spirit is Jesus' earthly agent (see John 16:13–15). The Spirit will equip the disciples with the presence of Jesus and the understanding of Jesus' teaching, as well as with the power to convict others when witnessing to the world. The Spirit is the surrogate of Jesus when Jesus leaves the earth. The Spirit is basically not an innovator, but by reminding them of Jesus' teaching leads the disciples into the truth already conveyed by the Son (14:26). The Spirit is seen as a source of continuing revelation for the disciples, a revelation ultimately going back to Jesus. When the disciples live in love, and thereby obey Jesus, they experience the love of God, through which they also experience the indwelling of God and Jesus. In 14:2–3 faith in Jesus leads to the disciples' communion with God and Jesus, whereas at 14:23 love of Jesus leads to the same end. To love Jesus is to live with God and Jesus—that is, to enter into relationship with them (15:9–10, 12).

The Spirit model of God in the Bible is broader than the specific Christian doctrine of "the Holy Spirit," which sees the Spirit as one aspect of God. In the Bible, Spirit is used comprehensively to refer to God's presence in creation, in the history of Israel, and in the life of Jesus and the early church. In addition to wind and breath, the Bible provides other non-anthropomorphic images, such as rock (meaning a place of refuge and safety). Additional non-masculine images include mother, wisdom, lover, and shepherd. These metaphors for the Spirit affect our root image of God in quite obvious ways: (1) they emphasize *the nearness of God* rather than the distance implied by the monarchical model, thereby suggesting the language of relationship; (2)

they utilize *both male and female metaphors* (as well as some that are neuter), and (3) they include *both anthropomorphic and nonathropomorphic images.* Taken together, these images suggest that the relationship to God is personal, even as God is more than a person. The sacred is not simply an inanimate mystery but a presence. Using an ancient biblical analogy, these metaphors lead to a covenantal understanding of the divine-human relationship, which emphasizes belonging and connectedness.

The images of God associated with the Spirit dramatically affect how we think of the Christian life. Rather than God as a distant being with whom we might spend eternity, Spirit—the sacred—is right here. Rather than sin and guilt being the central dynamic of the Christian life, the central dynamic becomes relationship—with God, the world, and each other.

Ultimately, spirituality is about one's relationship with God—not with an idea of God, but actually with God. While such a statement might seem mystical or unrealistic, it is both practical and realistic, if we understand God not as a concept or person, but as a stand-in for everything—Reality, truth, and the essence of our universe. What I have in mind, however, is not pantheism but panentheism, the view that God is in all things yet distinct and not a "thing" at all. What this means is that God is not simply another way of speaking of reality, for God is reality with a face—Reality with Personality—which is the only way most of us relate to others. For relationship to occur there must be personality.

The mystics of every religious tradition have always spoken out against specific definitions of God. The Western mystics appear to have assumed that a personal God was only a stage, and an inferior one at that, in human religious development. The mystical portrait of God was first imaginative, and then ineffable. It involved an interior journey, not an exterior one. In the mystical tradition, no one can claim objectivity for his or her insight. Each person is called to journey into the mystery of God along the pathway of his or her own expanding personhood. Every person is thus capable of being a theophany, as sign of God's presence; but no one person, institution, or way of life can exhaust this revelation. God, for the mystics, is found at the depths of life, working in and through the being of this world, calling all nature to its deepest potential.

In the past, traditional theologians preferred monarchical or hierarchical models of God, with the Father at the top, which then were imitated and promoted ecclesiastically and societally. If, however, as modern physicists such as Albert Einstein have noted, reality is dynamic rather than static, an energy field emerging from Mystery and flowing toward greater abundance and creativity, then God also is an energy field, flowing through us, to others. Such interflowing is the pattern of the universe, from atoms to galaxies, plants to animals, animals to humans, and humans back to everything else, all flowing from and toward God.

Many people today are finding the case for panentheism increasingly attractive in an age of science and reason. One can find historical traces of panentheism in both Western and Eastern orthodox theology, though the word itself was popularized by English philosopher Alfred North Whitehead (1861–1947). Panentheism is not the same as pantheism, the concept that "all things are God." Rather, pan*en*theism is the concept that "all things are *in* God." Panentheism views God not as a supernatural being separate from the universe, beyond nature and history, but as the encompassing Spirit around us and within us. According to this conception, God is more than the universe, yet the universe is in God. Viewed spatially, God is not "out there" but "right here." Whereas supernatural theism emphasizes God's transcendence—God's otherness, God as more than the universe—panentheism affirms both the transcendence and immanence of God. It does not deny or subordinate one in order to affirm the other. For panentheism, God is both more than the universe and yet everywhere present in the universe.

In our conception of the nature of God lies the kernel of the spiritual life. Until we discover the God in which we believe, we will never fully accept and understand ourselves. Such lack of acceptance and understanding means that the polarities of our nature will keep us frustrated and fragmented, preventing the wholeness and integration we seek and need for health and happiness. As we develop physically, intellectually, and emotionally, we must also grow toward a mature spirituality that includes reason, faith, and inner experience we can trust.

As individuals have their own unique way of interacting with the world, so also their conceptions of God. There is a place for each personality in the spiritual journey, a place for the religious thinker, the religious activist, the devotional practitioner, and the religious artist. There are many different ways of living the religious life and of experiencing God, each with its values, difficulties, and rewards.

Questions for Discussion and Reflection

In addition to the questions listed at the end of the preface, answer the following questions, writing your answers in a journal. If you are in a group study, be prepared to share your answers with those in the group.

1. Assess the author's statement that theology is not only about God but also about cosmology and anthropology.
2. Assess the validity and usefulness of Huston Smith's model of the four levels of the self and of their correlation with the four levels of reality.
3. In your own words, explain Smith's view of the difference between the soul and the spirit within the human self.
4. In your own words, explain Smith's view of the difference between the human spirit and the divine Spirit of God.
5. In your own words, explain Smith's view of the role of love as link between soul and spirit.
6. Assess the meaning and validity of the author's statement, "the process of coming to know or to experience God is also the process of loving oneself."
7. Explain both the problem and the necessity of personifying God and addressing God as person.
8. Explain and assess the meaning and validity of John Haught's proposal that we focus on "what" God is rather than on "who" God is.
9. Assess the merit of emphasizing neuter rather than masculine or feminine images in speaking of God.
10. Explain the meaning and implications of the statement that "God is Subject and not object."
11. Assess the merit of Martin Buber's notion that God be addressed as "Thou" rather than as "It."
12. Explain the distinction implied in affirming the word "God" as both verb and noun.
13. Asses the merit of the author's suggestion that we focus on the humanity of Jesus if we are to understand the meaning of his person, message, and ministry.

14. Assess the merit of the author's suggestion that the historical Jesus is best understood as both androgynous in spirit and by nature.
15. In your own words, explain the similarities and the differences between Jesus and the divine Spirit of God.
16. Explain and assess the merit of panentheism as an explanation of the nature of God and of God's role in the natural realm.

5

Holistic Happiness

As noted in chapter 2, pain, suffering, loss, and death are part of life, and there is no way to avoid them. American psychiatrist M. Scott Peck famously declared in his 1978 bestseller *The Road Less Traveled*, "Life is suffering," thereby agreeing with the fundamental teaching of Buddhism that because everything in life is transient, suffering informs the whole of life.

The Buddha compared his teachings to a raft, telling the story of a traveler who had come to a great expanse of water and desperately needed to get across. There was no bridge and no ferry, so he built a raft and rowed himself across the river. At this point in the story, the Buddha asked his audience what the traveler should do with the raft. Should he carry it on his back and lug it around with him wherever he went, or should he moor it and continue his journey? The answer was obvious. The same holds true with all religious and spiritual teaching. Its task is not to issue infallible definitions or to satisfy people's curiosity about metaphysical questions. Rather, its sole purpose is to relieve suffering and help people get across the river of pain to the further shore. Anything that does not serve the pragmatic goal of attaining peace, harmony, and well-being is of little importance and ultimately inconsequential.

From time immemorial, in every age, a set of questions emerge that uniquely define us as human beings: What's going on in the universe? Is there any point to it at all? Why am I here? Is there any purpose to my life? Is there a God? If so, why is there so much suffering? How can I find relief from suffering and sadness? Why do I die? What can I hope for? How should I live? These have been called life's ultimate questions. They are the ones that never go away.

It is the main business of religion to answer the big questions. And this is why, even when we try to distance ourselves from it, we remain intrigued by religion. Religion responds to the preoccupations that arise when life comes up against barriers beyond which ordinary—including scientific— ways of coping cannot take us. For our purposes, therefore, religions may be understood as pathways or "route-findings" through the ultimate limits on our lives. These limits include not only death and meaninglessness but anything that threatens our well-being, anything that stands between us and lasting peace or happiness.

Since the emergence of human consciousness, one question underlies all theological discussion and continues to be the burning theological issue of the day. Is there purpose to life? The Westminster Shorter Catechism utilizes traditional language to frame the question as follows: "What is the chief end of man?" The answer is clear-cut: "The chief end of man is to glorify God and enjoy God forever." In an earlier book, *Beyond Belief*, I proposed my own definition: "The purpose of life is to experience Life." I capitalized the word "Life" because by it I meant that "those who experience life fully experience God, who is Life."[1] I now wish to modify that statement, adding moral categories to my definition: *The purpose of life is happiness conducive to the equitable flourishing of all, for God is in all.*[2] In what follows I will support the claim that we live in a moral universe and that happiness can be achieved by following specific ethical principles.

Most human beings desire a good life. Thinking about a good life, how to achieve, maintain, and enhance it, occupies a great deal of our time and

---

1. Vande Kappelle, *Beyond Belief*, xviii.

2. Though I do not believe in a "personal" God, that is, in a God understandable to human beings and essentially viewed as an "overbig" person, I am not averse to using the term "God." The Bible, both in the Jewish and Christian testaments, declare that "God is Spirit," not person. It was with a metaphysical tradition of personhood in fourth-century Greek theology that calling God "person" took on some meaning. Today, because few of us are metaphysicians of that tradition, we would be better off dropping the notion of the personhood of God and finding a deeper understanding. When we cling to the concept of God as "person," we diminish God's transcendence. Monotheism is to God what a trunk is to a tree. We deceive ourselves if we imagine that the tree is the trunk or that the trunk, being the most visible element of the tree, is therefore the most vital. The tree would be nothing without its roots, which are diverse and rarely visible. In thinking of God, I suggest two metaphors: God is both everywhere to us, like water to fish, but also God is nowhere, like "the void" and "the silence."

Holistic Happiness

attention: we build comfortable homes and secure futures for ourselves; we work hard to advance in our careers; we seek to improve our health and expand our minds; we seek satisfying and enduring relationships with people who value similar goals and activities we enjoy. And because we live in community with others, we think about people whose lives have been shaken by war or violence or natural disasters, and we wonder how their needs relate to our lives.

Although Western ethical concerns have traditionally been voiced in Christian language, we know that this search for inner peace, integrity in relationships, and genuine care for other people is widely shared by our neighbors, whether or not they are Christian. While many people today, religious or secular, think of "the good life" in terms espoused by popular culture, namely as a life built around pleasant and interesting experiences, with enough money and leisure to meet personal desires and familial needs, few thoughtful people try to live a good life on entirely selfish terms. In fact, most of our neighbors of other faiths or of no faith would agree that the good life must include a concern for the well-being of others, peace between nations, and the health of our planet.

For Christians, this general understanding is sharpened by the teachings and example of Jesus, who often took generally accepted obligations and pushed them a step further, beyond what we originally thought. If the teachings of Jesus tell us about what makes a life good, they indicate that it sometimes involves putting the good of others ahead of our own:

> If you love those who love you, what credit is that to you? For even sinners love those who love them. If you do good to those who do good to you, what credit is that to you? For even sinners do the same. If you lend to those from whom you hope to receive, what credit is that to you? Even sinners lend to sinners, to receive as much again. But love your enemies, do good, and lend, expecting nothing in return. Your reward will be great, and you will be children of the Most High; for he is kind to the ungrateful and the wicked. Be merciful, just as your Father is merciful (Luke 6:32–36).

The Bible as a whole bears witness to the goodness of creation and its fitness for human habitation. If this is a world created as a place for human life, then our search for a good life has to be shaped in the context of a world that is shaped by love. As Robin Lovin indicates in his primer on Christian ethics, "Belief in God as the creator of a good world is less a narrative of how the world came into being than it is a fundamental confidence that we can live our lives in harmony with the natural world around us. . . . The search for a good life is not a struggle to wrest peace and happiness from a hostile or indifferent universe. Belief that God has created us for life in this world suggests also that human good is achieved by . . . a common life in which we may achieve a greater good together than any of us controls alone."[3]

Richard Coan, a professor of psychology at the University of Arizona, spent a large part of his professional career seeking to determine the nature of the optimal human personality. He provided a survey of his findings in his 1977 book *Hero, Artist, Sage or Saint?* Coan began by showing that psychology as a science cannot provide the goals for human life. He claimed that if any goals are provided by psychology, the psychologists must either introduce them surreptitiously or openly acknowledge the need for religion and transpersonal meaning.

Coan concluded that there are five elements that characterize the fully developed human person: efficiency, creativity, inner harmony, relatedness, and transcendence. As Coan described these elements, he defined efficiency as the heroic quality. Heroes accomplish things with effectiveness, have strong egos, and are able to focus the direction of their lives. The second element, creativity, is often represented by artists, who are able to present images, poetry, or ideas in a new way so that they touch others with a dimension beyond the physical. The third element is embodied by the sage, the person who has achieved inner harmony. The fourth element, relatedness, is manifested by the saint, the person who treats others with understanding, caring, love, empathy, social sensitivity, and compassion. Saints make other people feel loved and enable them to love. The fifth element is transcendence. This is the vertical aspect of saintliness, whereas relatedness may be considered its horizontal dimension.

Coan suggested that Carl Jung best integrated these concerns in his theory and practice, developing a framework in which all of these have a place. In a 1945 letter Jung wrote to P. W. Martin, a Quaker whose book *Experiment in Depth* was one of the first religious books to acknowledge the religious significance of Jung's work, Jung indicated, "You are quite right. The main interest of my work is not concerned with the treatment of neuroses but rather with the approach to the numinous. But the fact is that the approach to the numinous is the real therapy and inasmuch as you attain to the numinous experiences you are released from the curse of pathology."[4]

---

3. Lovin, *Christian Ethics*, 13.
4. Jung, *Jung's Letters*, 1:377.

For Jung, the human self is the creative principle at the heart of all reality, psychoid (spiritual) and physical. These two aspects of reality can be distinguished, although they interpenetrate one another. Jung usually referred to the spiritual realm as the psychoid. In his letters, he often spoke directly about God, but in most of his published writings he used less religious terminology, hoping to reach the scientific community. According to Jung, humans beings are related to and embedded in both the spiritual and physical dimensions of reality. Although he saw the place for behavioral, cognitive, existential, and Freudian therapeutic methods for healing patients, he was critical of these methods for claiming to offer exhaustive accounts of the human psyche and for neglecting important data found in the religious understanding of human consciousness. Jung's most important disagreement with non-religious psychological systems was his claim that while human beings are indeed physical creatures, we are also in touch with, surrounded by, and part of a meaningful nonphysical dimension of reality. He believed that unless humans come into touch with God, they are likely to become neurotic. He also believed that the religious and spiritual practice of the Christian church is the best therapeutic system available to human beings. Jung disagreed with those who saw evil only as the absence or deprivation of good. He was convinced that evil is a reality of experience with which humans are required to deal. He also believed that people who venture into the depths of the unconscious confront inner evil, and that they are helpless against it unless they are guided and guarded by a power greater than their own. For this reason, Jung devoted most of the last part of his life to understanding and describing the creative, restoring aspect of the unconscious, utilizing a framework quite similar to that of the New Testament and the teachings and practice of Jesus and of the early church. A remark that Jung made in a British Broadcasting Company Broadcast crystallizes his perspective: "Suddenly I understood that God was, for me at least, one of the most certain and immediate experiences . . . I do not believe; I know. I *know!*"

Ancient Wisdom Spirituality

From the earliest days of Christianity, the attraction and interaction of Christian theologians with pagan philosophy was pervasive. On the one hand, Gentile Christian theologians recognized their deep indebtedness to their Jewish heritage, with its historical and this-worldly emphasis. On the other hand, they were profoundly attracted to what we might call a higher spirituality—the soul's desire for higher things—one found in the Hellenistic philosophical tradition, with its allegorical and vertical concerns.

However, if one has nothing but pure allegory and a vertical spirituality, one would be gnostic, concerned with rejecting material things and becoming entirely spiritual. Such a stance implies rejection of the Jewish roots of Christianity. Thus, early intellectual Christians attempted to hold together both dimensions—the horizontal and the vertical—but to do so required a non-literal or allegorical reading of scripture.

When we explore the roots of ancient Gentile Christian spirituality, we turn to philosophy, for ancient philosophy was a form of spirituality, by nature religious rather than anti-religious. While ancient philosophers were skeptical of religious mythology, they were very much interested in the deeper truths believed to underlie mythology. Hence, pagan philosophers criticized Christianity, not for its religious nature, but because they believed they offered a better or higher spirituality. They blamed Christians for being too Jewish, meaning overly materialistic, too invested in natural and earthly pursuits.

In antiquity, educated Christians viewed philosophy as essential to a good education, much as we view the study of science today. Hence, Christian scholars and theologians were attracted to philosophy, and could not avoid interacting with it. The central themes of ancient philosophy were wisdom and happiness, stemming from the overarching philosophical question, "what is happiness?" To be clear, the Greek word we translate as "happiness" did not mean joy or pleasure, as we think today. Rather, happiness meant something like "true success or true fulfillment in life," closer to what today we call "the meaning of life." So the question, "what is happiness?" couldn't be answered by assuming that happiness is what makes us feel good, or even what makes us feel healthy, because such qualities are seen as means to an end, rather than ends in themselves. If feeling good or being healthy are the goals of life, it might be better not to be born at all, for good feelings or good health are at best temporary—and in the end, ephemeral.

While there were certainly hedonists in ancient times, such philosophies were not attractive to ancient Christians. Rather, learned Christians pursued the most widely accepted view of happiness among ancient philosophers, shared by Stoics, Platonist, and Aristotelians, namely, that happiness consists in a life of wisdom. In their estimation, wisdom was valuable for its own sake. Wisdom was the goal of all other values in life, whether money, power, or health; for ancient philosophers, pagan and Christian alike, all cultural values were secondary to wisdom.

Aristotle's *Nicomachean Ethics* was, in many ways, the first philosophical expression of what today we might call the "existentialist point of view." I say this because Aristotle's vision of the well-lived, and therefore the happy, life is achievable by the chosen actions of the responsible individual. What Aristotle's virtuous person consistently chooses is a course of action that is relevant to the situation, to oneself as a member of the human species but also to the unique here and now as a unique human being. Such behavior is what Aristotle called "the mean," that is, a chosen action that falls within certain parameters, avoiding extremes and yet appropriately tailored to the person as well as to the situation. What a particular person becomes is the result of the actions that person individually chooses. While the virtuous life is intrinsic to the well-lived or happy life, for Aristotle, this involved the assertion of the power of choosing as well as the development of practical wisdom necessary for such a life. Not everyone can be a philosopher in the full sense, but every person can and must be morally responsible if he or she is to live well—and no one can choose this for another person. Each person is thus responsible for his or her own happiness.

Long after Aristotle, the Danish Christian philosopher Søren Kierkegaard gave an interpretation of "the real self" that was both Christian and individualistic. For Kierkegaard, a well-lived life is one that is uniquely one's own, yet one that is also uniquely related to God, who knows and cares about each individual human being in the everyday affairs of his or her life. The central point he makes in his writings is that a life lived fully, authentically, and truthfully must be guided and empowered by a personal relationship with God. Each person is free to refuse this relationship, but to do so requires a terrible price. Kierkegaard called this price "despair" and "a sickness unto death," a death from which humans cannot die but that dooms them to live in a state of hopelessness and meaninglessness.

For Christianity in general, to become a person of wisdom requires both knowledge and understanding. The majority of ancient Christians, particularly those rooted in early Christian orthodoxy, gave biblical answers to philosophical questions. To the question, "What is happiness?" such Christians answered, "everlasting life," which in the Bible is not confined to life after death, but rather something realized in the present as well as in the afterlife. According to the gospel of John, "everlasting life" is to know God and Jesus Christ (17:3).

Holistic Happiness

Thus, for early Christian philosophers, happiness was the goal of life, and happiness consisted of a certain kind of wisdom, viewed as "the wisdom of God in Jesus Christ." To possess this wisdom was to possess everlasting life, and in order to possess happiness, Jesus Christ was the wisdom Christians sought. In 1 Corinthians, Paul calls Jesus "the power of God and the wisdom of God" (1:24). Early Christians noted that the Old Testament book of Proverbs spoke of wisdom as being in the beginning with God (8:22–31), and they found the same teaching in the gospel of John, where Jesus is called the Word with God in the beginning (1:1–5). Based on such correlation, early Christians naturally associated Jesus with God's eternal wisdom. For them, to know Christ is to know the wisdom of God, and to have happiness is to know Jesus Christ, the wisdom and power of God.

It is through the radical Jesus of the gospels as well as through the Holy Spirit that we touch God not as a concept but as a living reality. According to Zen master Thich Nhat Hanh, the beloved Vietnamese monk who for decades has lived in dialogue with Christianity, all human beings have the seed of the Spirit within them, meaning that each person has the capacity of healing, transforming, and loving. Through mindfulness—focusing deeply on the present moment—human beings can touch that seed and therefore touch God the Father and God the Son.[5] While Hanh has a deep respect for religious concepts, he views them as means, not as ends. Gently but firmly, he leads others from theory to practice, from concept to experience. Buddhism does not focus on faith but on practice. For example, Buddhists do not focus on nirvana, because nirvana means the extinction of all notions, concepts, and speech. Instead, Buddhists practice mindfulness, through sitting meditation, walking meditation, mindful eating, and so on. "Living mindfully, shining the light of our awareness on everything we do [is how] we touch the Buddha, and our mindfulness grows."[6] According to Hanh, "the living Christ" is present when Christians manifest Jesus by their way of life. When the church manifests understanding, tolerance, and loving-kindness, Jesus is there. In Buddhism, as in Christianity, practicing the teaching is the highest form of prayer.

---

5. Hanh, *Living Buddha, Living Christ*, 15.
6. Hanh, *Living Buddha, Living Christ*, 21–22.

The Right to Happiness

As mentioned above, I believe that the purpose of life is to seek happiness. Whether one believes in religion or not, whether one believes in this religion or that religion, we all are seeking something better in life. Thus, the very motion of our life is toward happiness. However, to understand the centrality of happiness, we must define what we mean by the term, for the concept of happiness is, at least in modern Western society, both elusive and ill defined. To define happiness, I return to the view of ancient Greek philosophers and early Christians that happiness is not so much a feeling as an entity associated with what we call "achieving meaning and purpose in life." Curiously, the English word "happy" is derived from the Icelandic word *happ*, meaning luck or chance. To the Western mind, it does not seem the sort of thing one can develop or sustain. Properly understood, however, happiness can be achieved, but only by a certain inner discipline, by undergoing a transformation of our outlook, attitude, and approach to life. Simply stated, we need to identify those factors that lead to happiness and those factors that lead to suffering. Once we do this, we can set about gradually eliminating those factors that lead to suffering and cultivate those that lead to happiness.

According to Eckhart Tolle, the author of the bestselling *The Power of Now*, happiness should be dissociated from life's external conditions, whether positive or negative, and be relegated solely to "inner peace," a nondualist perspective that functions in perfect equanimity beyond pain and suffering and lives "in complete acceptance of what *is*." According to this view, there is no "good" or "bad" in life, there is "only a higher good—which includes the 'bad.'"[7] While I accept the view that there is "a higher good beyond good and bad," I want to make sure that we don't limit Tolle's concept of "inner peace" to mental or emotional states only, but understand it in a wider holistic sense as involving external as well as internal factors, as an overall acceptance of well-being that includes peace of body, mind, and spirit.

A good place to start in the journey to happiness is with the question of purpose. What is the purpose of your life? What makes your life meaningful? Whatever your answer, no one chooses to be unhappy, meaning that somehow happiness is central to the issues of personal meaning and purpose. At this point you might wonder, isn't a life based on seeking personal happiness by nature self-centered, even self-indulgent? Not

---

7. Tolle, *Power of Now*, 178.

necessarily. As spiritual and psychological studies demonstrate, unhappy people tend to be most self-focused and socially withdrawn. Happy people, by contrast, are generally found to be more sociable, flexible, and creative, able to tolerate life's daily frustrations more easily than unhappy people. More importantly, happy people are found to be more loving and forgiving than unhappy people are.

We begin, then, with the basic premise that the purpose of our life is to seek happiness. It is a vision of happiness as a real objective, one that we can take positive steps toward achieving. While most of us tend to assume that happiness is determined primarily by external events, that is highly unlikely. Rather, the reverse is true; happiness is determined more by our state of mind than by circumstances or events in our lives. Success may result in a temporary feeling of elation, and misfortune might well send us into depression, but sooner or later our overall level of happiness migrates to our customary level of happiness. Studies demonstrate that winners of state lotteries respond predictably at first, but the initial high eventually wears off and the winners return to their baseline level of happiness. The same occurs to those who are struck by catastrophic events, for after an appropriate adjustment period, they typically return to their normal or near normal level of day-to-day happiness. That is because our moment-to-moment happiness is largely determined by our outlook. In fact, whether we are feeling happy or unhappy at any given moment often has little to do with our overall condition, but, rather, is primarily a function of how we perceive our situation, that is, how satisfied we are with what we have.

As the Dalai Lama notes in his book *The Art of Happiness*, the Buddhist tradition identifies six factors of fulfillment or happiness, namely, good health, wealth, friendship or companionship, worldly satisfaction, spirituality, and enlightenment. While all of these factors are sources of happiness, in order to be able to utilize them fully, our state of mind is key. For example, if we harbor hateful thoughts or intense anger somewhere deep down within ourselves, then it ruins our health, and thus destroys one of the factors. Also, if we are mentally unhappy or frustrated, then physical comfort is not of much help. On the other hand, if we can maintain a calm, relaxed state of mind, then we can be very happy even if we have poor health. However, even if we have great wealth or wonderful possessions, if we are experiencing anger, hatred, or envy, at that moment these mean nothing. At such times, even friends can be annoying or distant.

Holistic Happiness

Furthermore, we often confuse desire with purpose. Some desires, however, are more connected with purpose than others are. For example, the desire for happiness is always right, as is the desire for inner peace, including a friendlier and more harmonious world. Anything we can do toward those ends is beneficial and satisfying. At some point, however, desires can become unreasonable, such as desires to own and possess unnecessary objects. If you feel you need something, ask yourself whether you really need it. The answer is usually "no." If you follow that initial impulse, very soon your desires will increase and your level of satisfaction will decrease. The demarcation between a positive and a negative desire or action is not whether it gives you an immediate feeling of satisfaction, but whether it ultimately results in positive or negative consequences. Excessive desire generally leads to greed, and if you reflect upon greed, you find that it leads to feelings of frustration and disappointment rather than to satisfaction. The true antidote of greed is contentment. If you have a strong sense of contentment, it doesn't matter whether you obtain the object or not, for either way, you are still content. Of course, the most reliable method in life is not to have what we want but rather to want and appreciate what we have, for closely linked with an inner sense of contentment is an inner sense of self-worth. When a person has a sense of dignity and self-worth, there is less chance of that person becoming depressed, and hence less chance of risking and loosing what he or she already has.

As should now be clear, happiness should not be confused with pleasure, which is momentary and transitory. Spiritual maturity, often associated with wisdom, liberation, and enlightenment, has proven over time to produce genuine, lasting happiness, for by enhancing one's self-worth, happiness produces better health and well-being while eliminating a great deal of mental, emotional, and even physical suffering.

Christopher Reeve, an established Hollywood actor famous for playing the role of Superman, injured his spinal cord in 1995 after falling off his horse in an equestrian competition. As he approached a triple pole jump, his horse stopped and Reeve fell headlong across the barrier. The blow left him paralyzed from the neck down and confined to a wheelchair for the rest of his life. As doctors later revealed, had he fallen one centimeter further to the left, he would have died on the spot. If he had fallen further to the right, he would most likely have walked away with less than a concussion. A phrase from his wife later gave the name of his memoir (*Still Me*): "You're still you. And I love you."

Reeve became an inspiration, not only for his efforts to overcome his injury, bur for his work on behalf of people living with paralysis. In 1999 he established a foundation that raised over $130 million for research intro treatments, increasing public awareness for the difficulties of those living with disability. It is important at such times to have an anchor that undergirds our life. I would suggest the best anchor is that provided by the presence of God in our lives, who created us for a purpose, and who loves and accepts us unconditionally.

Training the Mind for Happiness

If happiness can be achieved through training the mind, we need to learn what emotions and behaviors are harmful and which are helpful. This also involves awareness of which emotions and behaviors are harmful to society and to the future of our planet. Through the process of leaning we gradually develop a determination to change what we can, beginning with our emotions and behavior. In Buddhism, the principle of causality is accepted as a natural law. Thus, for instance, in the case of everyday experiences, if there are certain types of events that are not desirable, then the best method of ensuing that they do not occur is to ensure that the causal conditions that normally give rise to that event no longer arise. Similarly, if we want a particular event or experience to occur, then the logical thing to do is to seek and perpetuate the causes and conditions that give rise to it.

For example, hatred, jealousy, and anger are harmful states of mind, and these emotions should be dealt with decisively. On the other hand, mental states such as kindness and compassion should he affirmed and cultivated. When we treat others kindly and compassionately, most often those around us react in kind. Such attitudes create a sense of trust and intimacy with others that creates kinder and more constructive neighborhoods in society. As a byproduct, states like kindness and compassion lead to better psychological health and happiness. Instead of categorizing moral actions as sinful or virtuous, it might be better to speak of them as positive or negative as to whether they lead to suffering or to ultimate happiness.

In training the mind for happiness, it is important not to think of one simple secret or key to happiness. Like proper eating, the approach must be holistic, that is, involving body, mind, and spirit. Change takes time, and negative states of mind, built up over a lifetime, are particularly stubborn. For this reason alone, we need external help, help from mentors and friends as well as from God. In addition, we need to implement valuable moral and religious principles and practices, starting with small and manageable changes. Eventually, as we gradually emphasize positive practices, the negative emotions and behaviors are automatically diminished. Through commitment and training and the calming of our minds, eventually we can change and experience significant emotional and spiritual transformation. Gradually, the effects of negative efforts on our minds will lessen and remain on the surface, like waves that may ripple on the surface of an ocean but have little effect deep down.

The systematic training of the mind—cultivating happiness, genuine inner transformation, and challenging negative mental states—is possible because of the very structure and function of the brain. We are born with brains that are genetically hardwired with certain instinctual behavior patterns, and are predisposed mentally, emotionally, and physically to respond to our environment in ways that enable us to survive. These basic sets of instructions are encoded in countless innate nerve cell activation patterns, specific combinations of brain cells that fire in response to any given event, experience, or thought. However, the wiring in our brains is not static, nor is it irrevocably fired. Rather, our brains are adaptable. Neuroscientists have documented the fact that the brain can design new patterns, new combinations, of nerve cells and neurotransmitters in response to new input, and this is true regardless of our age. In fact, our brains are malleable, ever changing, reconfiguring their wiring according to new thoughts and experiences. As a result of learning, the function of individual neurons themselves change, allowing electrical signals to travel along them more readily. Scientists call the brain's inherent capacity to change "plasticity."

Ethical training is another feature of the kind of inner discipline that leads to happiness. Great spiritual teachers of all the world's religions advise followers to perform wholesome actions and avoid indulging in unwholesome actions. Whether our action is wholesome or unwholesome depends on whether that action or deed arises from a disciplined or undisciplined state of mind. It is felt that a disciplined mind leads to happiness and an undisciplined mind leads to suffering.

When I speak of discipline, I am referring to self-discipline imposed by a desire to fulfill our individual potential, not discipline that is externally imposed on us by others. In this case, we are focusing on the discipline necessary to overcome our negative qualities and behavior. All humans require education and self-discipline to fulfill their potential, and this applies to happiness and well-being as well. When it comes to attitudes and behavior, many of us become despondent, believing these are the results of genetics or socialization. To some extent this is true, but equally true and significantly so is our innate desire to avoid suffering and gain happiness. However, these can only succeed through education, training, and discipline. To come naturally, wholesome thought and behavior, like unwholesome ones, can only gain traction through practice.

Unlike institutional Christianity, which tends to emphasize the doctrine of original sin, mature Christians need to focus on original goodness. Such a view affirms that human nature is fundamentally good, gentle, and compassionate, rather that sinful, rebellious, and destructive. Changing our self-image through learning, reinforcement, and understanding can have a lasting impact in how we conduct our daily lives and interact with others.

For proof of our innate goodness, we have only to look at our emotional nature, which seems more suited to gentle, loving, and compassionate states of mind than to compulsive, aggressive behavior. Indeed, a calm, affectionate, wholesome state of mind has beneficial effects on our health and physical well-being. Conversely, feelings of frustration, agitation, and anger can be destructive to our health. There is no question that affectionate attitudes and other gentle emotions help stabilize our personalities while contributing greatly to happier family and community life.

Of course, conflicts and tensions do exist, not only within our individual minds but also within our families and our interaction with others on a societal, national, and global level. Anger, violence, and aggression do arise in our developing egoic nature, but they can be exacerbated as a result of immaturity or by abuse and insecurity experienced during childhood and later formative years. Thankfully, given the development of human intelligence, we are able to rely on inner wisdom and discretion to avoid or to conquer adverse emotional conditions. If our moral and emotional intelligence develop in unbalanced ways, without being counterbalanced with nurture, compassion, and support, our actions can become destructive. However, where human intelligence and human goodness work together, all human actions become constructive. When we combine an affectionate spirit with knowledge, education, and positive reinforcement, we also learn to respect the rights and views of others.

Despite the influence of philosophers like Thomas Hobbs and psychologists such as Sigmund Freud, who saw human nature as inclined to aggression and the human race as violent, competitive, and concerned only with self-interest, contemporary research demonstrates that humans have an underlying tendency toward altruistic behavior, a pattern particularly evident among disaster victims, who counter trauma by working together. Medical doctors and psychological research have discovered that the risk factors for coronary heart disease increase among people who are most self-focused. Additionally, they are discovering that those who lack close social ties seem to suffer from poor health, are more vulnerable to stress, and exhibit higher levels of unhappiness. It is now also becoming clear that when children are exposed to the right conditions, such as having parents who are able to regulate their own emotions, who model caring behavior, who set appropriate limits on their children's behavior, who communicate that children are responsible for their own behavior and who use reason to reinforce affection or positive emotional states, these will enable the innate seeds of goodness and compassion to flourish, thereby heightening their child's sense of self-value and the family's overall well-being and happiness.

Compassion is the awareness of a deep bond between oneself and all creatures. Once we conclude that the basic nature of humanity is compassionate rather than aggressive, our relationship to the world around us changes immediately. Seeing others as basically compassionate instead of hostile and selfish helps us relax, trust, and live at ease. And it makes us happier.

Seeing human nature as primarily compassionate leads naturally to the conclusion that the purpose of life is happiness. That simple affirmation then serves as a powerful tool in helping us navigate through life's daily problems. From that perspective, our task becomes one of discarding those things that lead to suffering and embracing those things that lead to happiness. Practicing the presence of happiness gradually increases our awareness and understanding of what truly leads to happiness and what doesn't. In this regard, many of us need to practice the Welcoming Prayer, which helps us find serenity in the messy moments of life. When we feel triggered or caught by something unpleasant, we implement this prayer by being present to our feeling. This happens when we welcome anger, fear, or anxiety as mentors. In your prayer, welcome everything that comes to you today: welcome all thoughts, feelings, emotions, persons, situations, and conditions, knowing that they are for your healing—for the restoration of your happiness. When you do so, you are letting go of aggression, of your need for power and control, letting go even of your desire for esteem, approval, and pleasure. By letting go of your ego needs, you open up to the presence of God, to God's grace, love, power, and action within.

Holistic Happiness

When life becomes too complicated and we feel overwhelmed, it is useful to stand back and remind ourselves of our overall purpose, on what bring us happiness, and then reset our priorities on the basis of our goal. This can put our life back on track, allow a fresh perspective, and enable us to see which direction to take.

From time to time we are faced with pivotal decisions that can affect the entire course of our lives, including decisions regarding getting married, having children, embarking on a course of study in preparation for a career, and making plans for retirement. The firm decision to become happy—to learn about the factors that lead to happiness and take positive steps to build a happier life—can be such a decision. Turning toward happiness as a valid goal and consciously deciding to seek happiness in a systematic manner can profoundly change the rest of our lives. For our life to be purposeful, we must develop innate human qualities such as warmth, kindness, compassion, and optimism. Then our lives become meaningful and more peaceful—happier!

Questions for Discussion and Reflection

In addition to the questions listed at the end of the preface, answer the following questions, writing your answers in a journal. If you are in a group study, be prepared to share your answers with those in the group.

1. In your own words, explain the meaning and significance of the Buddha's raft analogy.
2. Of the "big questions" mentioned at the start of the chapter, which do you find most perplexing or least satisfactorily explained by traditional world religions? Explain your answer.
3. If you were asked to answer the question, "what is your chief purpose or end in life?" how would you answer?
4. Assess the validity of the author's definition, "The purpose of life is happiness conducive to the equitable flourishing of all, for God is in all."
5. In your estimation, do we live in a "moral universe," or is morality merely a human construct? Explain your answer.
6. Of the five elements selected by Richard Coan that characterize the fully developed human person, which, in addition to "transcendence,"

Holistic Happiness

do you hold paramount in your scale of human qualities? Explain your answer.

7. Assess the merit of Carl Jung's view that the religious and spiritual practice of the Christian church is the best therapeutic system available to human beings.

8. Assess Carl Jung's view of evil as an actual metaphysical reality that has lodged itself in the depths of our unconscious selves, and that human beings are helpless against it without divine assistance.

9. Assess the merit of the author's view that "ancient philosophy was a form of spirituality."

10. In your estimation, how do the writings of ancient Greek philosophers such as Aristotle help us understand the concept of happiness, and how did they distinguish happiness from pleasure?

11. Define and assess the early Christian definition of the concept of happiness.

12. If you were asked to define the concept of happiness in personal terms, what would you say? Does your definition include the issue of meaning or purpose in life? Why or why not?

13. Assess the notion that the mind can be trained for happiness. In your estimation, if such training were possible, would the resultant inner happiness be momentary or truly lasting? Explain your answer.

14. If you identify with traditional Christianity, do you endorse the notion of original sin or focus on original goodness instead? Explain your answer.

6

Holistic Loving

WE HUMANS ARE CERTAINLY strange creatures. We spend limitless time on unimportant things and little time on some of the most crucial areas of our lives. For example, we spend twelve years in school learning to read and write and picking up enough math to balance our checkbooks and budget our lives. Some of us go on to college to learn the fundamentals of a career or a profession. We also spend hours and weeks and months learning to play sports or games such as chess or bridge. However, we seldom spend much time in learning about human beings and how we can get along with them. Oddly, though we spend much time preparing for our careers, we spend little time preparing for marriage, raising children, and coping with illness, disappointment, and old age. And yet our mental health and happiness, and even our life expectancy, depend to a large degree on how well we have learned about ourselves and other human beings, and how to relate to them.

Jungian Personality Theory

One of the most important contributions of Swiss psychiatrist Carl Jung to modern psychological thought is his theory of personality types. While Jung's monumental study, *Psychological Types*, requires a good deal of psychological and philosophical background to be understood, the essentials of his theory have been elaborated and developed by others, including the personality type indicator developed by Isabel Briggs-Myers and her mother Katherine Cook Briggs known as the Myers-Briggs Type Indicator (MBTI), which charts sixteen possible personality types in terms of Jungian type theory. Today, thanks to this sorting device, many Jungian concepts are widely known and accepted and millions have taken the MBTI, which is widely applied in team building, organization development, business management, education, and career and marriage counseling. Understanding one's type is making a welcome change in people's lives globally, in a wide diversity of situations.

The MBTI, now available online, is not really a test, but a sorter of preferences on four scales or categories, each consisting of two opposite poles. At the conclusion of the test you receive four letters, which comprise your personality type. They indicate the differences in people that result from

- where they prefer to focus their attention (Extraversion or Introversion)—E or I;
- the way they prefer to take in information (Sensing or Intuition)—S or N;
- the way they prefer to make decisions (Thinking or Feeling)—T or F;
- how they orient themselves to the external world (Judging or Perceiving)—J or P.

These preferences produce sixteen different kinds of people, interested in different things and drawn to different fields. Each type has its own inherent strengths as well as its likely blind spots. However, these types often blend into one another, inasmuch as each of us is a unique combination of these attitudes and functions. Discovering one's personality type is extremely beneficial, for it influences career choices, marriage choices, learning style, spiritual journeys, theological understanding, and much more. Learning one's personality type also makes us more aware and sensitive to the psychological needs, preferences, and differences of those around us.

If we are to care for, work with, or love other people, we need to know what makes them unique, and we will need to help them develop their own type potential and relate to them in ways that are meaningful to them. For example, people with developed sensate functions are usually characterized by simplicity in life style. They are interested in concrete facts and seldom in fantasy or make-believe. The basic interest of the intuitive type is in acquiring wisdom. Unlike sensors, they are fascinated by fantasy, hunches, and imaginative possibilities. However, routine tasks often bore them and they often do not follow through. They need new challenges, new problems, variety, and change. The thinking type wants things understandable

Holistic Loving

and in logical order; consequently, thinkers do not like exceptions to rules. Often they make good executives, because the good of the whole takes precedence over individual desires. They can make decisions, but sometimes their apparent coldness alienates other types. The feeling type is most often characterized by an ability to experience joy. It is important to realize that the word "feeling" does not mean emotion, but rather signifies the capacity to evaluate data according to human values. Feelers are interested in other human beings and what influences them. They are excellent at getting along with others and are often found in the helping professions. Making unpleasant decisions affecting the lives of others is difficult for them.

Of the two middle letters in one's type (S or N, T or F), one will be the dominant function, the home base of operations, and the other will be the auxiliary, one's second most important function. It is impossible to love others unless we can recognize their type and place an adequate value upon their primary function. But here's a caveat: We should never try to have other persons change their type. They will do best if they develop what they are by nature.

When people are young, their energy is directed toward development of their most preferred, dominant function, and their behavior reflects this. For example, an introverted Feeling child will be a quiet observer, with an instinctive sense of others' feelings; an introverted Intuitive child will be actively exploring the variety of the surrounding world. An extraverted Thinking child will try to order his environment to fit with his logical principles; an introverted Thinking child will try to internally make sense of her world. Once children develop skills in their dominant function, the focus of energy and attention then shifts to the auxiliary function. The primary task of type development in the first part of life is to establish the leadership provided by the dominant function, balanced by the healthy development of the auxiliary function. Later in life, the focus of development shifts, this time to the less-preferred functions, aspects of the individual's personality and potential that have only minimally been explored. This redirection of energy is part of the midlife transition, which Jung saw as the gateway to later life development and satisfaction. The task of the second half of life, then, is to move toward full development of all of oneself, including those parts that were previously neglected and unrealized.

When people first learn Jung's theory, they often think the ideal is to develop all four functions with equal facility to achieve balance. That, however, is not how development works, for if a person tries to develop opposite ways of perceiving equally, for example, then neither Sensing nor Intuition will receive the focus or attention necessary to become fully reliable. The four functions tend to pull in opposite directions: Sensing, to the reality of the present; Intuition, to the possibility of the future; Thinking, to decisions based on objective logic; and Feeling, to decisions based on subjective values. People who do not establish dominance of each pair of functions are inconsistent in their behavior, pulled first in one direction and then another. The goal of type development, then, is not equal development and use of all the functions, but rather the ability to use each mental process with some facility when it is appropriate.

In conclusion, Jung's model of the human journey is based on the following assumptions:

- each person has an innate urge to grow
- the human psyche is self-regulating and capable of healing itself
- development means developing conscious control over and facility in the use of a function
- development is an interaction between a person's innate type preferences and the environment. If the environment is supportive, growth tends to follow innate type. If the environment is not supportive, the pattern may be affected by a person's adaptation to the requirements of the environment
- in the first half of life, growth takes the form of development of the preferred functions; in the second half of life, a person's focus of energy and attention naturally shifts to the less-preferred functions. This is a process of moving toward one's unexplored potential.

The following quote summarizes Jung's understanding of the psychological-spiritual task during the second half of life: "Among all my patients in the second half of life—that is to say, over thirty-five—there has not been one whose problem in the last resort was not that of finding a religious outlook on life."

The Need for Intimacy

Our need for other people is paradoxical. At the same time that our culture is caught up in the celebration of fierce independence, we also year for intimacy and connection with friends and loved ones. In the West, there is a certain type of relationship that is valued above others, namely, having one special person with whom one can share one's deepest feelings, fears, and so on. In fact, people in Western societies often feel that unless they have a relationship of this kind, that there is something missing in their lives. Virtually all researchers in the field of human relationships agree that intimacy is central to our existence. It is clear that intimacy promotes both physical and psychological well-being. In looking at the health benefits of intimate relationships, medical researchers have found that people who have close friendships, people whom they can turn to for affirmation, empathy, and affection, are more likely to survive health challenges such as heart attacks and major surgery and are less likely to develop diseases such as cancer and respiratory infections.

Intimacy is equally as important in maintaining good emotional health. The psychoanalyst and social philosopher Erich Fromm claimed that humanity's most basic fear is the threat of being separated from other humans. He believed that the experience of separateness, first encountered in infancy, is the source of all anxiety in human life. While connection with others is difficult to achieve, mature spirituality values such intimacy, but also invites maintaining closeness with as many people as possible. In fact, the aim is to connect with everyone one meets.

So, given the vital importance of intimacy, how do we set about achieving intimacy in our daily lives? A good place to begin is with a workable definition. While researchers agree about the importance of intimacy, studies on intimacy reveal a diversity of definitions and theories. While some specialists define intimacy by emphasizing physical or bodily contact, other investigators, stressing the Latin root *intima*, meaning "inner" or "innermost," define intimacy as the desire to share one's innermost self with another. Others, stressing the underlying need or desire for closeness, accentuate diversity among humans, meaning there are infinite variations among people with respect to how they experience or demonstrate the sense of closeness. However defined, intimacy offers humans a great opportunity, for it means that at this very moment we have vast resources of intimacy available to us and through us.

While there is a widespread notion in our culture that deep intimacy is best achieved within the context of a passionate romantic relationship, this view can be profoundly limiting, for it cuts us off from other potential sources of intimacy, and it can be the cause of much misery and unhappiness when that Special Someone isn't there. If what we seek in life is happiness, and intimacy is an important ingredient of a happier life, then it clearly makes sense to conduct our lives on the basis of a model of intimacy that includes as many forms of connection with others as possible.

A good place to begin in cultivating connectivity with others and in reducing conflict with them is empathy, namely, by developing our ability to appreciate another person's pain and suffering. Empathy, an important part of compassion, requires the capacity to suspend insisting on our own viewpoint and the ability to look from the other person's perspective, to imagine what it would be like to be in their shoes, and how we would deal with this. This helps develop an awareness and respect for another's feelings, which is an important factor in reducing conflicts and problems with other people.

Whenever we meet other people, it is helpful to approach them from the standpoint of what we have in common. We each have a physical structure, a mind, and emotions. We are all born in the same way, and we all die. All of us want happiness and do not wish to suffer. Other persons have the same capacity for experiencing pain, joy, happiness, and suffering that I do. Looking at others from this standpoint rather than emphasizing secondary differences such as race, religion, or cultural background allows us to sense that in meeting others, we are meeting people much like ourselves. It is also helpful to understand and appreciate the background of persons with whom we are dealing. Being curious, open minded, and honest are useful qualities when it comes to dealing with others.

Recent studies support the idea that in addition to making a more peaceful and equitable world, developing compassion and altruism have a positive impact on a person's physical health and well-being. One study found that doing volunteer work on a regular basis, interacting with others in a warm and compassionate way, dramatically increases life expectancy and overall vitality. Studies in the field of mind-body medicine demonstrate similar findings, documenting that positive states of mind can improve one's physical health.

In addition to the beneficial effects on physical health, there is evidence that compassion and caring behavior contribute to good emotional health. Studies also show that reaching out to help others can induce a feeling of happiness, a calmer mind, less depression, and enhanced self-worth. There is a great deal of loneliness in our world, and empathy and compassion necessarily create a feeling of affinity and interconnectedness.

Holistic Loving

The Centrality of Love

Over the years I have become convinced that love is the central reality in our universe, and that our primary task as human beings is to know this love and to express it to those around us. Paul stated this idea incomparably in the thirteenth chapter of his first letter to the Corinthians. While the description he provides of love is certainly inspirational, it is important that his teaching come alive specifically and concretely in our lives.

In *The Road Less Traveled*, M. Scott Peck speaks of love from his many years as a practicing psychiatrist. He recognizes that when we attempt to speak of love, we are in the realm of mystery. "In a very real sense, we will be attempting to examine the unexaminable and to know the unknowable. Love is too large, too deep ever to be truly understood or measured or limited within the framework of words. . . . In an effort to explain it, therefore, love has been divided into various categories: eros, philia, agape; perfect love and imperfect love, and so on. I am presuming, however, to give a single definition of love, again with the awareness that it is to be in some way or ways inadequate. I define love thus: The will to extend one's self for the purpose of nurturing one's own or another's spiritual growth."[1]

Ultimately, love is an experiential reality. We either experience it or not; we either know what it is to be loved and to love, or we know little or nothing of love. Those who have never known what it is to be loved or have never tried to love others can no more define what love is than the blind can expound on the many shades of red. Incidentally, if we would know God, we had best discover the experience of love, for none of us can know or love God until we have experienced love to and from another living being. As psychologists, pastors, and counselors acknowledge after years of listening to people, when therapists get beyond the superficial questions and fears, longings and doubts, they find that most clients are seeking to be loved and to love.

All the great religions of the world speak of the importance of love. Indeed, as the world's mystical literature reveals, a recurrent topic is the mysticism of love. In Taoism and Confucianism, human beings are not following the Way or the Tao if they are not compassionate or caring. Buddhism speaks of bodhisattvas who deny themselves the bliss of nirvana in order to return to help others find release and fulfillment. Many Hindus worship the savior god, Ganesha, who is the heart and soul of compassion,

---

1. Peck, *Road Less Traveled*, 81.

rather than Shiva and Kali, the primordial masculine and feminine deities. The followers of Islam are constantly referring to Allah as the all-merciful and compassionate. Additionally, Judaism includes in its scriptures graphic love poetry known as the Song of Songs.

Yet despite this emphasis, no great religion places love as consistently in the center of its thought and practice as Christianity. While the church, being a human institution, has often failed to live up to the message of its founder and its scripture, and so-called Christian culture is far behind the church, where Christians have lived close to the spirit of Jesus of Nazareth, they have been called saints, and the chief characteristic of their sainthood has been their knowledge of God as love and their expression of that love in their lives through concrete actions of compassion and empathy.

There is little question that love was considered central by Jesus and by those who were closest to him, as well as by those who have followed him most closely through the centuries. In the gospel of John, Jesus summarized discipleship best when he said, "I give you a new commandment, that you love one another. Just as I have loved you, you also should love one another. By this everyone will know that you are my disciples, if you have love for one another" (13:34–35). The essential distinguishing sign of being a follower of Jesus is found in manifesting or showing forth the kind of love and caring that Jesus had for his disciples. In a passage in the Sermon on the Mount, Jesus extends this love to all human beings and distinguishes his teaching with the proviso to "love your enemies," for by so doing, you will be children of your Father in heaven, who "makes his sun rise on the evil and on the good, and sends rain on the righteous and on the unrighteous" (5:44–45). It would be difficult to make love more central to the human condition than this.

The author of the first letter of John writes, "God is love, and those who abide in love abide in God, and God abides in them. . . . Those who say, 'I love God,' and hate their brothers or sisters, are liars" (4:16, 20). Paul also talks constantly about the centrality of love. Not only does he write a hymn of praise about love in 1 Corinthians 13, but in his letter to the Romans he writes, "Owe no one anything, except to love one another, for the one who loves another has fulfilled the law" (13:8). Of course, the love of which the New Testament speaks has little to do with feelings of love. The love it describes is not satisfied just being an emotion. It continues to love other human beings until they feel loved and cared for by us. Such love is a

Holistic Loving

mixture of caring and action. Indeed, those who love participate in God's way of reaching out to humanity.

In the Old Testament, we find love emphasized, although not primarily as in the New Testament. Hosea takes a prostitute as his wife and forgives her repeatedly as a living symbol of God's enduring love and patience for his people Israel. In Leviticus we are told to love God and our neighbor as ourselves. Jesus picks up this theme of love found in the Old Testament and makes it central to his teaching and practice. In Mark 12:29–31 Jesus indicates that the Great Commandment is "'Love the Lord your God with all your heart, and with all your soul, and with all your mind, and with all your strength.' The second is this, 'You shall love your neighbor as yourself.' There is no other commandment greater than these."

While much conventional and popular Christianity gives the impression that it is wrong to love oneself, this is incorrect, for we cannot come to the full potential of which we are capable until we love, and that potential begins with love of oneself. While it is easy to confuse genuine caring for ourselves with selfishness and egotism, they are different. Selfishness and self-love, far from being of the same class or category, are actually opposite. Truly selfish people not only have difficulty loving others, but they seldom love themselves either.

The medieval mystic Meister Eckhart clearly understood the difference between self-love and selfishness when he stated, "If you love yourself, you love everybody else as you do yourself. As long as you love another person less than you love yourself, you will not really succeed in loving yourself; but if you love all alike, including yourself, you will love them as one person and that person is both God and man. Thus he is a great and righteous person who, loving himself, loves all others equally."[2] Carl Jung tells an illustrative story about one of his patients who sought an appointment with him only to be told by Jung that his schedule was full during a specific week. During that week this patient was sailing on a lake near Jung's house and saw Jung sitting on the wall at the back of his home, with his bare feet dangling in the water. At the next visit with Jung the patient was bitter, complaining that Jung had lied to him, to which Jung replied, "No, I had an appointment with myself, one of the most important ones I ever have."

As we begin to love ourselves and value what we are in spite of our faults and failings, then we are free to like other people and treat them with loving concern. Once we come to have a genuine regard for ourselves, then

---

2. Eckhart, *Meister Eckhart*, 204.

we don't have to be on the defensive by drawing attention to the faults of others. In addition, we don't have to protect our egos with a shield of gossip or anger. Nor need we any longer be worried that others may be talking about us. We know how we stand with ourselves and that we are trying to do our best; what others say won't add or subtract from that assessment. Consequently, we no longer need to be hurt over slights or injuries because we know that other people probably didn't mean them—and even if they did, it was a piece of poor judgment on their part. If we can lovingly accept what we are and what we are trying to become, we can see that the negative opinions of others are simply misunderstanding on their part. The uninformed opinions of other people no longer bother us. Then a wonderful thing begins to happen. We begin to forget about ourselves and turn to other people and think about them and what concerns them and how we can show them love.

In Leviticus 19:18 we read that we are to love our neighbor as ourselves. Jesus pointed out that the obvious implication here, that we cannot very well love our neighbor unless we love ourselves. Before we jump to conclusions and misunderstand the implications here, it is important that this teaching contradicts the doctrine of the total depravity of human beings, for while there is in each of us a combination of light and dark, there is also great potential in every human being. To truly love oneself is to acknowledge the light and the dark, the True Self and the False Self, including one's shadow side. To face ourselves fully and honestly allows us to control our negative and destructive parts without giving way to despair.

People who only see the good in themselves are actually quite dangerous and capable of the worst havoc. While it is impossible to pray and meditate effectively without bringing all of ourselves before God, so too we cannot love ourselves unless we know ourselves fully, the good and the bad, and what is within us to love.

As we begin to see what is within us, and take responsibility for what we find, we begin to take charge of our life. Each of us has a certain amount of freedom to develop a consistent pattern of action by picking a goal and working to make it the central direction of our life. It is our task to choose among the elements that we find within ourselves and decide which of them we wish to express and which not to express. Choosing who we need to become is essential toward being a loving person. Furthermore, there is in each one of us something priceless and eternal. If we think of ourselves as unworthy, we may well be rejecting the love of God, who knows and loves us unconditionally. It is just as morally wrong to dislike, despise, and devalue ourselves as it is to have these attitudes toward others. Perhaps it is worse, since doing so is refusal to accept God's love for us. The first step toward self-love, then, is a simple one. We need to make a conscious decision to see ourselves through the eyes of the Divine Lover.

The next step in loving ourselves is learning to accept forgiveness from others. For some people, it is far easier to forgive than to be forgiven. In the Sermon on the Mount, Jesus was specific in telling his disciples the importance of accepting forgiveness. There he emphasizes that if we have done anything to our neighbor for which we did not attempt to receive forgiveness, or for which we did not accept forgiveness, then we are to leave our gifts before the altar and seek forgiveness (see Matt 5:23–25). The Christian church is built on those who accepted forgiveness and loved God the more for it. Peter denied Jesus, and Paul persecuted the risen Christ and tried to destroy his church. Both accepted the forgiveness of God and became founders of the church.

In developing our spiritual goals and direction, one of the most important things for those who would grow in love of themselves is to find a fellowship of caring people with whom to relate. In addition, each of us needs spiritual friends with whom we can discuss all aspects of our lives. The capacity to love others seldom, if ever, grows in a vacuum. Ideally, the church is supposed to be a fellowship filled with compassion, understanding, and the love of Christ. If it were really such an accepting fellowship (rather than the handful of isolated individuals who happen to gather for worship), then miracles of transformation would happen.

The next step in trying to come to self-acceptance is being honest with ourselves. As Christian counselors frequently note, most people feel guilty for the wrong things. They judge themselves for the wrong mistakes, attitudes, and vices. Often sexual peccadilloes are considered far worse than the more serious sins of pride and arrogance. Until we can look at ourselves with objectivity, it is nearly impossible for us to see what is good and what needs changing in our life. There is no point in despising ourselves for actions for which we don't need forgiveness. In this regard, we need to distinguish between hang-ups and sins.

As we welcome the Lord into our soul room, we find that he laughs and talks with us, and tells us that he is with us through thick and thin, in good times and in bad times, and that we are to go out and treat others as he treats us. As we do, we look at our soul room and notice it has been transformed. As the Lord leaves, he turns and says, "Thank you for letting me come into your life and give you meaning and value. I am with you here whenever you wish me. Love yourself and others who need your love, as I have loved you."

It is in such moments of prayer that we find it easier to love ourselves. It is with this new sense of peace and desire that we are to go out and love others, supportive in their joys and compassionate in their sorrows.

The Art of Listening

It is impossible for us to love other people unless we listen to them. We simply cannot love without learning to listen. The kind of listening I am talking about is listening that does not judge or evaluate. It is open, objective, and attentive. Listening is important because each person is unique. Just as there are different types of people, so all have different value systems. Each of us is shaped by different positive and negative circumstances, and no two human beings are formed in the same mold. Genuine love is always centered in the need of the other person and in ministering to that need. It is not a matter of giving what we feel like giving, nor is it about furthering our agenda. How can we possibly provide someone care and understanding unless we know that person? And how can we know others unless they disclose, reveal, or unveil themselves to us? When we try to love without first knowing the needs of those around us, we are likely be to ministering to our own needs and not to theirs. Without listening there is little communication, and without communication there is little love.

One indication of the small amount of listening there is in our society is the high price that psychologists and psychiatrists demand. And they will be the first to tell you that much of all psychotherapy is simply warm, receptive listening. Let us be clear: There is a vast difference between letting another person unload and true listening. We can dump our problems on our barber or hairdresser, but that is neither effective listening nor true communication. It is also true that the very people who are closest to us are the ones to whom we listen the least. This is particularly true of the busy and overworked American family.

If listening is as important as it appears to be, it requires learning and discipline. The following steps have proven beneficial in learning this skill. First, we need to talk less. We obviously cannot listen until we stop talking. However, it is one thing to cease constant chatter and quite another matter to learn to listen. Real listening is being silent with another person or group of persons in an active way. Many people are shy or using chatter to cover their true issues or concerns. True listeners are those who are quiet and yet sensitive toward others, and who do not allow their minds to wander or to daydream. Listening is not coercive or overbearing, for listening gives freedom and does not need to control what is heard or need to censor it. When listening to others, we need to be aware of body language, ours and theirs. It is nearly impossible to listen until we have started accepting ourselves, and once we can accept all of us, the good and the bad, once we are able to put aside our illusions about ourselves, then we can begin to listen because we will not be shocked or upset by what we hear.

People caught in illusions about themselves cannot even read books with which they disagree. They fight the authors in order to protect their illusion, and so they get little value from what they read. Listening to others is not so different from listening to books. Many people cannot bear to hear ideas or actions with which they disagree. They fear that they condone whatever they hear. So they dare not listen without reaction, emotional and verbal, without vociferous dissent. Our very ability to listen compassionately, then, is a sign that we are achieving some inner security.

Listening also involves patience. Others need to reveal themselves at their pace and not at ours. As Morton Kelsey noted in his book *Caring*, as professor and counselor at the University of Notre Dame, he listened to one young man once a week for three school years before that student trusted him enough to reveal what he considered the deepest stain on his soul. Listening creates a deep bond between persons, and it is not always a one-way street, for creative listeners need not always remain silent. Rather, they need to respond, not only through body language and verbal reflection, but also in ways that express understanding and empathy. Real listening is warm, interested, and concerned. It seeks to know and to care, for it is love in action.

In listening, the bottom line seems to be whether the other person feels he or she is being listened to. As I mentioned above, listening is not a one-way street. Listening often involves sharing ourselves. In doing so, however, we need to make sure the roles have not been reversed, unless, of course, it is listening between good friends, in which the obligations to listen are mutual. We need to keep in mind that only rarely are we allowed into the deeper levels of a human's soul unless we have first listened to the more superficial levels of other people. Genuine listening must be honest and authentic, for people seldom reveal deep pain unless they know that we are open to all of them. Listening to people on this level brings us to love those who have revealed themselves to us, for we experience them as God-bearers and their soul as holy. Listening on this level is a kind of prayer, for it penetrates through the human being and comes to hear the Spirit of God that dwells in each of us. Real listening can be a religious experience, for we have entered a holy place and have communed with the heart of Being itself. Indeed, seldom do we develop the capacity for listening to the still small voice of God until we have first learned to open ourselves to other human beings. Finally, in thinking of listening skills, we need to remember that listening requires privacy and confidentiality.

The task of listening is the same as that of loving: to enable others to grow, take responsibility for their lives, form their own value system, and come to their own full potential by their own choice.

Loving Family, Friends, Enemies, and Strangers

There are many people in our lives and in the world, and we certainly need to be selective as to whom we should listen. If we are married, the list begins with our spouse and children, for these are our primary objects for care and love. The evidence is in, that the most significant factor in the development of children is the quality of the family life in which they are raised. It is quite obvious and understandable that the attitudes and values of children spring from their family life. As love breeds love and kindness breeds kindness, so violence stimulates violence, and indifference fosters indifference and apathy. It is also understandable that mental stability and health are the product of a loving environment just as mental illness is often the tragic result of a lack of love during the first years of life. Even physical stature and bodily stamina are influenced by the kind of family life people have had and the amount of love they have received.

In interactions with parents, children, and spouses, it is imperative that men and women value one another equally, even as they should maintain the value of children. The ancient world believed that men were the heads of each household. Women existed to bear children and to minister to the needs of men. Women were not believed to be men's equal physically, mentally, morally, or religiously. Since women were considered inferior to men, it followed that men felt that they should rule the family with complete authority.

It is important to know that Jesus did not agree with this view of family life and relationships, and neither should we. Such lack of dignity, respect, and equality did not accord with what Jesus knew about human beings and about God. No one had more to do with the breakdown of this purely masculine attitude toward the family than Jesus did. Just as his teaching about the basic moral equality of human beings and their equal worth before God finally bore fruit in the abandonment of slavery, so too his teaching about the family would ultimately end masculine domination of family life. Although most of what Jesus said about women, children, and family life is held in principle by most Western culture, the actual practice is far different. It took eighteen hundred years before his ideas about slavery took root, and his ideas about women and children have still not taken root among many Christians.

While loving everyone is a great ideal, it is important to realize that we cannot love humanity in general until we learn to love individuals, and there is no better place to begin than with those who are close to us (spouse, children, and parents as well as friends, community members, and acquaintances at work, play, and school). In addition to listening, another way of showing love is by simple acts of kindness and thoughtfulness, acts that are sacramental extensions of our love. Again, such acts begin at home, and then by extension, to those around us.

If we want to express love to family and friends, it is important that we stand up for them when they are subjected to condemnation or criticism, whether from others or from themselves. Our acceptance and praise are much more likely to provide strength, direction, and guidance than picky judgment and continued harping about what is wrong. Parents often make the mistake of thinking that they must produce fine, perfect children solely by their direction and discipline. Hence, as adults, many of us our likely to treat those around us in the same way. However, everyone needs a place where they are accepted and considered valuable, whether they are right or wrong, and a real friend, parent, or spouse is one who stands with us whether we are right or wrong, just because they love us. My experience is that I seldom help others by judging them; I merely add to the burden of guilt they are already carrying. The opposite of judgment and criticism is not looking the other way, but rather looking for potential in the other person, dwelling on the positive and creative rather than upon the negative.

In the Old Testament book of Leviticus, the Israelites were told to love all other Israelites in these words: "you shall love your neighbor as yourself" (19:18). Jesus, however, took this statement from the Torah and gave it a greatly expanded application. In Luke 10 we are told that an expert in the law tried to trap Jesus by asking him what course of action was necessary to obtain eternal life. Jesus replied with the classic Hebrew summary of the law: you must love God and your neighbor as yourself. When the scribe, in order to justify himself, asked, "And who is my neighbor?" Jesus told the story of the rescue by a Samaritan of a Jew who had fallen among thieves. One important point of this story is that all human beings are our neighbors, even our most despised enemies. Ancient people were taught to love their friends and families with great passion and devotion and to hate their enemies with an equal hatred. In the Sermon on the Mount, Jesus clearly taught the opposite: "You have heard that it was said, 'You shall love your neighbor and hate your enemy.' But I say to you, Love your enemies, and pray for those who persecute you . . . For if you love those who love you, what reward do you have? Do not even the tax collectors do the same? And if you greet only your brothers and sisters, what more are you doing than others? Do not even the Gentiles do the same? (Matt 5:43–44, 46–47). Jesus believed that real ascent on the spiritual way does not begin until we start to love our enemies, those who mistreat us or spitefully use us. This does not mean that we are to love the enemy instead of the friend or family member, but in addition to them. Loving those who are near is a preparation for this supreme effort.

One conventional way of avoiding the strong medicine of the gospel of love is to maintain that we can love people but don't need to like them. Let me say clearly and simply, loving without liking is not loving at all. Genuine love is a quality of caring that finds something appealing in the other person as well as makes the heroic effort to "love." To follow the way of love all the way to the cross was the way of Christ, for whom loving and liking converged. This does not imply that we approve of everything that other people are doing, for they may be causing harm and hurt. But we can still care for them and love them.

The first step in our attempt at loving the enemy is to realize that we have enemies, people whom we do not like and who respond in kind. Loving our enemy, however, like pain, has a great mentoring effect, for it teaches us not only how selective our love can be, but also how little caring there is in most of us much of the time. It is easy to find fault in others, such as prejudice, selfishness, and narrowmindedness, but it is not so easy to acknowledge equal faults within ourselves. We turn again to the message of the gospel, and remember that Jesus told his followers that they should turn the other cheek and go the second mile with one who forces them to go one mile. In other words, if we are to grow in love, we simply have to cease our own destructive actions before we can focus in the right direction. One of the reasons that the Christian church conquered the ancient world was that it actually practiced loving strangers and forgiving the enemy. The martyrs went to the arena without cursing and breathing vengeance upon the spectators. Often the spectators at the arena were stupefied, and eventually, many were won over to this astounding faith.

Jesus also placed an incredible emphasis on loving the stranger and reaching out to the neglected. In Matthew 25 we find Jesus identifying with the forgotten and marginalized of society when he said, "I was hungry and you gave me food, I was thirsty and you gave me something to drink, I was a stranger and you welcomed me, I was naked and you gave me clothing, I was sick, and you took care of me, I was in prison and you visited me" (25:35–36). In thinking of the stranger, we become aware of others, and realize how much we think of ourselves and our circle, our clique, our reactions and desires. As we become aware of others, we start thinking of those who are different from ourselves, of those who need our friendship. Like the ancient Israelites who needed to be reminded that they were once strangers in the land of Egypt (see Lev 19:34), we too need to be reminded of the times when we felt lost and alone. At such times we recall one of the greatest teachings of Jesus, known as the Golden Rule: "do to others as you would have them do to you" (Matt 7:12; Luke 6:31). Most of the evil in this world is caused not by wicked people but by unconscious people, by the very lack of awareness that lets us ignore others.

Sometimes when we see the enormity of the problems on earth we become so overwhelmed that we are paralyzed and don't know where to begin. That's when we need to stop and ask ourselves how our love reaches beyond our inner circle of family, friends, and acquaintances and out to the strangers whom we have never met. Which human need tugs at our heart? Which burden seems to be laid upon us? Is it racism? Is it the prison system? Is it the system of justice that seldom sends any but the poor and underprivileged to prison? Is it migrant laborers, or those destroying themselves with drugs, or battling the crippling effects of disease? Or is it perhaps ministering to the person who is depressed or easy to ignore in our own suburban society? Misery is misery wherever it is. Christian love with its eyes open will reach out in concrete ways to human agony.

Ultimately, it is impossible to develop faith unless we have been loved, for faith is a byproduct of love. How can we believe that there is a God who cares and watches over us until we have experienced this love from some human being and are thereby given a vision of the love that dwells at the core of reality? And seldom is it possible to have hope without having been nurtured with love. Love gives life meaning. How can we hope for good in the future unless we have known something of it in the past and present? Without having been loved, there is little to look forward to, and nothing to imagine as the fulfillment of life.

Love creates peace within the soul. Peace is not resting or inaction; it is rather the harmony of all things working together in their proper place. Beyond happiness is joy. Joy is creative satisfaction that seeks to give of itself to others. Joy is the result of having been touched by human love and being led by it to Divine Love. In writing to the Corinthians asking that they settle their differences in love, Paul painted a picture of what truly loving persons look like: "Love is patient; love is kind; love is not envious or boastful or arrogant or rude. It does not insist on its own way; it is not irritable or resentful; it does not rejoice in wrongdoing, but rejoices in the truth. It bears all things, believes all things, hopes all things, endures all things" (13:4–7).

Questions for Discussion and Reflection

In addition to the questions listed at the end of the preface, answer the following questions, writing your answers in a journal. If you are in a group study, be prepared to share your answers with those in the group.

1. The MBTI, designed as a self-sorting way to determine one's personality type and to learn how one's preferences on a variety of important factors influence your interests and behavior. If you have taken the test in a relaxed and unpressured environment, the results should be accurate, intriguing, and relevant. If you have taken the test, were you pleased with the experience and confident in the results? I you have not taken it, I encourage you to do so at your earliest convenience.

2. Because preferences can change over time, you should retake the exam every five to ten years. If you have retaken the MBTI, did your results change? If so, how? If not, why not? NB: It is likely that the results of your testing will change when you move from the first to the second half of life spirituality.

Holistic Loving

3. Assess the author's statement that intimacy is central to human health and well-being.
4. In your estimation, how are intimacy and happiness connected? Explain your answer.
5. Explain the role of empathy, compassion, and altruism for good health and well-being.
6. Assess M. Scott Peck's definition of love as "the will to extend one's self for the purpose of nurturing one's own or another's spiritual growth." If you find this definition too narrow or constricting, what changes would you make to have it conform to your definition?
7. Assess the author's statement, "none of us can know or love God until we have experienced love to and from another living being."
8. In your estimation, is it possible to love one's neighbor as oneself? Explain your answer.
9. Assess the meaning and validity of Meister Eckhart's statement, "If you love yourself, you love everybody else as you do yourself."
10. Assess the author's statement, "The first step toward self-love is . . . to see ourselves through the eyes of the Divine Lover."
11. After reading this chapter, what did you learn about the art of listening?
12. After reading this chapter, what did you learn about loving family and friends?
13. After reading this chapter, what did you learn about loving enemies and strangers?

7

Holistic Work

ACTIVE PEOPLE DO NOT live in a vacuum. We live in the world, interact with society, have job concerns, money problems, social disagreements, and security issues. In addition, we live with prejudice, racism, sexism, classism, intolerance, poverty, pollution, the disintegration of the family, corporate greed and scandals, unemployment, and widespread job dissatisfaction. Through it all, we need a way to be happy at work as well as at home, and that is not always easy.

Research studies indicate that there is widespread dissatisfaction at work. One recent survey reported that nearly half of American workers are unhappy with their jobs; and things seem to be getting worse. The reasons are varied, ranging from inadequate compensation and boredom to core complex factors related to the specific nature of the work or to workplace conditions. All sorts of things can make someone unhappy at work, including poor social atmosphere, lack of recognition, and monotony. Many workers complain that they lack autonomy, that is, freedom to do their work in their own way. Conversely, others complain that they don't get enough information and direction from their bosses.

Of course, no boss or supervisor can control a worker's attitude. We can all choose to utilize certain inner qualities or spiritual strengths to change our attitude at work or toward bosses and co-workers. Nevertheless, if there is injustice and exploitation, then passive toleration is the wrong response. The appropriate response is to resist it by trying to change the environment rather than accept it. However, if we know there is a higher purpose to our work, and we know that we are doing something useful for society, then that can have a positive effect on our attitude.

In today's workplace environment there is often a focus solely on productivity and on bigger profits. This type of environment leads to much inequity, unfairness, and stress on the employees, and workers must ponder their alternatives. Sometimes we tend to think in black-or-white terms about our jobs, and we must realize that no situation is 100 percent good or 100 percent bad. Everything in life is relative, and it helps to cultivate a wider perspective of the situation. Some jobs may have higher pay, but they come at a price, including longer hours, more responsibility, and possibly risk of injury. When we consider the larger picture, we may discover that while our current work pays less than others, it may come with certain advantages, such as less demands and less danger.

In all cases, contentment is the key. If you have a poor job and the skills and qualifications for better work, then by all means you should exert your best effort for a better job or for a promotion in your current job. However, if you are earning enough to support your family and for your survival, then you need to consider the good aspects of your current situation and realize that you are better off compared to many others. In such situations, a good question to ask is, "Am I permanently happier from the last promotion I received?" Additionally, "Are people situated at higher positions in my place at work happier than those in lower positions?" As recent studies show, people with better paying jobs or more important jobs are no happier in life than those with less important jobs. Surprisingly, findings indicate that while job satisfaction is linked with life satisfaction, the specific type of work one does, including one's occupational prestige, or whether one is blue collar or white collar, has little impact on one's over-all life satisfaction.

Furthermore, if we take a large enough view of things, we notice that all things are interconnected. Often problems in the workplace are caused by factors beyond our control. Perhaps some worldwide economic condition or even certain environmental problems are at the root of the problem. In these cases, it does no good to take things personally. If we feel angry and direct it against others in the workplace, our anger or frustration may only make us more bitter and yet have no effect on the situation or change the wider problems. When workers focus on the larger issue, it creates a sense of unity among them, which creates a sense of greater satisfaction instead of the divisions and conflicts caused when they lose sight of the wider issues and start complaining among themselves. Instead of misplaced anger and frustration, it helps to turn our mental energy in a more constructive direction. This may take some time, but meantime if we can't change the work environment, then we may need to change or adjust our outlook. Otherwise we will remain unhappy at work and in life.

The Correlation between Social Interaction and Job Satisfaction

In virtually every study of workplace conditions and the factors that contribute to employee satisfaction or dissatisfaction, the social climate of the organization plays a prominent role. It is of little surprise, therefore, that in our discussion of happiness at work, sooner or later we are bound to touch upon the subject of relationships at work, how we interact with one another, and whether we are able to maintain basic human values such as compassion, human affection, and treating others with warmth, honesty, and sincerity.

It is important to note when talking about human values that these are not simply ethical or religious subjects. Compassion, respect, and sincerity are not important because some religious text says they are, but because our very happiness depends on them. Positive states of mind have clear benefits to our physical, mental, and emotional health, not only at work or at home, but also for the ultimate benefit of society. At work, if we have a warm spirit and display human affection, our mind will be calmer and more peaceful, which will give us the ability to function better, increasing our judgment and decision-making abilities. In this case, whatever kind of work we do, it can be a source of satisfaction. Then we can look forward to going to work, and be happier there. Have you ever noticed how you feel when someone is polite, kind, or simply gives you a genuine smile? It makes you want to respond in kind. This shows how one person can influence another's attitude, which implies that one person can make a big difference. In fact, one person can change the atmosphere of a workplace environment. For example, you can see what happens in a tense group of co-workers who don't get along. If a new employee shows up, one who is warm and friendly, after a while the mood and attitude of the whole group changes for the better. Conversely, sometimes when people at work are getting along and are friends, if someone new starts work, someone who is a troublemaker, that person can affect the whole group and cause conflicts and problems. Hence, each of us can have an effect on others, and have the ability to change the atmosphere at work.

Holistic Work

In his book *The Art of Happiness at Work*, co-written with the Dalai Lama, psychotherapist Howard Cutler notes the influence of two checkout clerks at his local supermarket. Jane, a woman in her mid-thirties, goes about her job efficiently and quickly, yet she rarely says a word other than calling out for a price check, and she seems always to have a slightly sullen expression on her face. Dorothy, another clerk, a happy lady in her late fifties, regularly engages customers in friendly banter, always smiling and helpful. She asks them about their lives and remembers what they say. One day the bagboy offered to push Dr. Cutler's cart to his car, and on the way they spoke about the older clerk, at which the bagboy declared, "When Dorothy is working, everybody seems to be in a better mood, even the manager. I'm not sure why, but things just seem to go better on the days that she's working."[1]

In thinking of the importance of the human factor at work, a good place to begin is by recognizing that all workers are interdependent; they all depend on one another for their livelihood. Normally, it is natural to think of ourselves as independent and separate from others. That feeling probably affects young people more than others, for among the young there is the tendency to think that one can manage alone and is not dependent upon others. However, no matter what kind of job we have, there are co-workers who contribute to the running of the company that we depend on for our livelihood. Without them, the company simply would not exist, and we would not be able to earn a living, not to mention our customers, suppliers, or the many others who make it possible for us to earn money.

In addition, when we are faced with hostile co-worker or unreasonable supervisors at work, a wider perspective can sometimes help—realizing that this person's behavior may have nothing to do with us, for there may be other causes for their behavior totally unrelated to us. In such cases, it is important to cultivate a deeper compassion for others; ideally, that compassion should be unbiased, that is, directed toward everyone equally. If we look deeply at others, no matter how rich, famous, powerful, or nasty they might be, they are still human beings just like us, subject to the changes of life, old age, illness, loss, and so on. Even if it is not apparent on the surface, sooner or later we will recognize that they are subject to suffering, and that their very humanity makes them worthy of compassion. In this regard, it is helpful to note that when people are in conflict with one another, or complaining about their supervisors or bosses, we must be willing to see them as deserving of compassion as any other human being.

1. Dalai Lama and Cutler, *Happiness at Work*, 42.

Finally, it is possible to regard situations of stress and perplexity in our workplace as opportunities to train our mind and spirit and to cultivate spiritual values such as compassion, patience, tolerance, and forgiveness. It is a wonderful thing if we can use our place of work as a place of spiritual growth and practice as well. Of course, practicing patience and tolerance should never mean that we should passively allow ourselves or others to be harmed in any way—in those cases, we need to take appropriate countermeasures. However, there are many examples of people who have been imprisoned and tortured, some as political prisoners, who were able to use their spiritual practices even in these extreme conditions, and in some cases even strengthen their spiritual practice while maintaining compassion even toward their captors.

Compensation Satisfaction

According to a Gallup survey, Americans generally tend to be more satisfied with the social aspects of their job than they are with matters of recognition. For many people, their salary or pay are viewed as an objective measure of how much they are valued by an employer. However, in today's society, our pay level often represents more than that. It not only reflects how much we are valued by the employer, but it also can be linked with our sense of self-worth. Such evaluation, nevertheless, illustrates an important principle.

If we choose an external marker as the measure of our inner worth, whether it is the amount of money we make, or others' opinion of us, or the success of some project we are involved in, sooner or later we are bound to be assaulted by life's inevitable changes. After all, money comes and goes, and thus is an unstable source of self-esteem, an unreliable foundation upon which to build our identity. Despite this, no matter what kind of work we do, according to social scientists, around one third of American workers see financial rewards, rather than the nature of the work itself and its primary purpose, as the most important aspect of their jobs. These people are particularly prone to intense resentment and dissatisfaction if they feel that they are unfairly compensated for their efforts.

Of course, there is nothing wrong with making money. In a modern industrial society, people need to find their own way of making a living, meaning that our attitude toward work as primarily a source of livelihood is very realistic, particularly if we have a family and children to support. The problem occurs when the motivation to make money becomes an end

Holistic Work

in itself. When this happens, we lose sight of the very purpose of making money, which is a means to a greater purpose. The problem with pursuing money simply for its own sake is that this makes us victims of greed, which produces a never-ending cycle of need, with which we are never satisfied. In this case, we become slaves of money. If such pursuit actually succeeded in making us happy, that might serve a commendable purpose, but that is rarely the case. In fact, the real problem is that in this game of gain, someone is always ahead of us, and we never have enough. If we make a million, we want ten million, and then a hundred million. Thus, unless we learn to say when something is enough, we are never truly content. This is like a game where the goalpost is constantly being shifted so that we never have a chance to win.

Some people pursue money not for the things it can buy but for the power it gives. However, authentic power results not from what we are worth but rather from the respect that people give. Real power, like that found in Jesus, Mother Teresa, or Mahatma Gandhi, has to do with one's ability to influence the hearts and minds of others. Power based on wealth is artificial and not lasting. If we lose our money, the power and respect vanish. It's like the power based on someone holding a gun—as soon as they put down the gun, there is no respect or power given them.

Another great motivation for making money is the underlying belief that the richer we are, the more freedom we have. In this case, we have freedom to travel where we want, as well as freedom from the burdensome worry about adequate food, clothing, and shelter. Surely people need a certain amount of money to live happily, but beyond that, it can actually be hindrance. A better reason to make money is because of the difference it can make when shared with people struggling to survive. However, some problems are simply too big for our charitable contributions. In these cases, it would be more helpful if we volunteered with causes that raise awareness or consciousness about such things as poverty, injustice, and global warming.

When it comes to happiness, however, it is important to be aware that rich people are not necessarily happier than poor people; in many cases, they are actually more miserable and unhappy than their less fortunate counterparts. As studies show, once people have their basic needs met, having more money doesn't bring greater happiness. In fact, according to an article in *The New York Times*, real income rose over 16 percent in America during the last thirty years of the twentieth century, but the percentage of Americans who described themselves as "very happy" actually fell from 36 percent to 29 percent during the same time period. Interestingly, that same survey showed that the largest decline in satisfaction came from those with the highest income.

Of course, people must decide for themselves how much money they need, but if such people shared their wealth, they would actually be happier, for they would have more friends, better reputations, a more positive legacy, and even less regret when they died. At least they could say to themselves, "I used my money to help others." If people's happiness and self-worth are based on the creation of wealth, then they end up perpetuating a cycle that leaves them forever unhappy. However, if they realize that money is important, but that other factors are equally or likely more important than wealth, such as compassion, justice, and mercy, then they would likely be happier and more contented.

Unless we exist in abject poverty or are suffering from hunger or starvation, our attitudes about money are more important than the amount we make. As always, in our pursuit of happiness, our inner resources assume a greater role than our material resources. In his book *Authentic Happiness*, Martin Seligman, one of the key figures in the study of human happiness, states, "Our economy is rapidly changing from a money economy to a satisfaction economy." He asserts that in many individuals' choice of work, personal satisfaction focuses on financial rewards as the determining factor. He points out, for instance, that while law is now the highest paid profession in America, for many people money alone is no longer enough to entice them to enter and continue the practice of law. In fact, in major cities across our country, law firms are now spending more on keeping their staff than on recruitment, as many attorneys are abandoning the practice of law for kinds of work that may not pay as much but that will make them happier. This attitude is also trending in other professions as well.

Boredom and Lack of Challenge in the Workplace

Boredom and lack of challenge have long been identified as common sources of dissatisfaction at work. To enjoy maximum work satisfaction and performance, workers must find a balance between two poles—with too much challenge on one end and not enough challenge on the other. With too much challenge, workers experience stress, strain, and deterioration of work performance. With too little challenge, workers become bored, which inhibits job satisfaction and hinders performance.

Holistic Work

In my case, first in my role as teacher and then as writer, I overcome tedium by adding new material in my courses and by challenging myself to introduce new courses and write about new and challenging topics. Looking back, I realize that the harder and more challenging the level of work I have been asked to perform or have asked of myself, the greater my satisfaction has been. So even though hardship and stress are rarely welcome in the moment, they regularly result in increased levels of happiness, satisfaction, and self-worth. Whether it be mental work or physical work, for progress, development, and personal growth to occur, challenge is necessary. As people who have gone to college and then on to higher levels of academia know, students have to spend many hours developing and presenting points of view, and then having their views challenged by professors and peers alike. I remember hearing how in the past, yeshiva students training for careers as rabbis and interpreters of Jewish legal and religious texts were paired up in teams of two, each individual required to take a point of view on a passage of scripture or on a legal principle and defending it under intense scrutiny. Following that, each would take an opposing view on the same passage or scripture and defend it under challenge. By engaging opposition, a deeper understanding of one's position emerges. If people think only about their own viewpoint and have no willingness to open themselves to opposing viewpoints, there is little room for growth or improvement. Challenge and opposition produce growth physically, mentally, and spiritually, and are essential to all education and training, both for career and for life.

In his highly influential *The Wealth of Nations*, Adam Smith wrote that people who spend their lives engaged in the same repetitive task tend to lose "the habit of exertion" and generally fail to improve. The reason is simple: in challenging circumstances, our creative nature is fully engaged and fully utilized. Scientific research clearly shows that human beings tend to be more dissatisfied without the element of challenge. Thus, if we are confronted with work that doesn't challenge us, our minds are free to cultivate spiritual practices and explore ways of responding to others with kindness, empathy, and compassion. Of course, given some people's personality needs, social situations, and overall levels of stress, unchallenging work might be more therapeutic than challenging work, reducing rather than increasing worry, accumulated stress, and frustration. This is where individual variation comes into play; people differ in the degree of challenge they require or are willing to meet. Some people thrive on highly challenging work, while others may be less willing to take on challenging work. So, as we seek to optimize our

Holistic Happiness

happiness at work, it is up to each of us to decide what level of challenge provides the greatest degree of growth and satisfaction. Whatever our circumstance, it is important to relate to co-workers with love and affection rather than with indifference or disdain. Treating others with respect and engaging them with affection is always a rich source of satisfaction. In fact, life offers many such moments of satisfaction, moments that can arise effortlessly and spontaneously. This sense of fulfillment can occur anywhere—and of course, the workplace should be included.

One of life's great experiences—whether at home, at work, or at play—is a condition called "flow." The term "flow," first introduced in the late twentieth century, describes a mental state that most of us have experienced at one time or another. To be in flow means to be totally absorbed in whatever one is doing at the moment. It occurs when one is fully present and completely focused on the task at hand. Essentially, flow can occur during any human activity, whether at work or at play, and in all types of physical, mental, social, and spiritual activity.

Flow arises when we engage in activities we feel are important, meaningful, and worth doing. Flow more likely occurs when there are clear-cut goals to the activity and when we receive feedback about our progress as the activity unfolds. The task must be challenging and require skill, and there must be a proper balance between the challenge and our capabilities. People in flow feel that their skills are fully engaged in the task at hand, and even though the project may be challenging and require skill—at that moment it feels effortless. While in flow, people are engaged in an activity for its own sake and not for any external rewards they might receive.

In whatever task people perform, whether required or self-imposed, each person can develop the capacity to focus attention on any chosen object or activity for prolonged periods of time. One of the characteristics of such a focused mind is its total absorption in the chosen activity. In most cases, even disturbances in the immediate environment have little or no effect in one's depth of concentration. When people are in the state of flow, whether at work or at play, they are not thinking about how happy they are or how much fun they are having. The sense of satisfaction comes later. Of course, one can't be in this state all of the time, but it can be maintained over a sustained period of time. While this flow state is not reliable or sustainable, it can become a great source of satisfaction in one's work, along with shaping one's outlook and attitude. According to a Gallup poll, around one fifth of American workers report experiencing some degree of flow on a daily basis, with flow defined as being so completely absorbed in work that one loses track of time. However, more than one third of workers polled indicated that they rarely or never experience it.

When talking about human happiness, whether at work or at play, we need to distinguish between two types of human satisfaction: pleasure and happiness. Pleasure can certainly provide a temporary kind of happiness and engender intense emotional states. However, pleasure arises on the basis of sensory experiences, and since it depends on external conditions, it is an unreliable source of happiness. True happiness relates more to the mind and heart. Happiness that depends mainly on physical pleasure is unstable, but happiness that is associated with a sense of meaning and arises on the basis of deliberately cultivated attitudes and outlooks is lasting. Such happiness may take longer to generate, and requires effort, but it is this lasting happiness that can sustain us even under the most trying conditions of everyday life.

Thinking about the flow state, while it produces a sense of happiness we might call gratification or fulfillment, it is not necessary or even effective in motivating us toward personal or emotional growth. Happiness is something we can choose and cultivate, and unlike pleasure, which is ephemeral, true happiness can be lasting. It is definitely possible for us to have routine work, work that might not be challenging and might even be boring, and yet be happy. The world is filled with examples of individuals who have sources of satisfaction and fulfillment that sustain them under all sorts of conditions. While some people may be workaholics, in that they thrive at work and in their careers, a happy life should have variety and not be based solely on job or money.

For those who find work tedious or boring, there is the principle of adaptation, an innate feature of being human that has been thoroughly studied and documented by psychologists. The principle of adaptation suggests that no matter what kind of success or good fortune one experiences, or, alternatively, no matter what adversity or tragedy one encounters, sooner or later people tend to adapt to the new conditions and eventually migrate back to customary levels of happiness. Thus, someone could be promoted to CEO unexpectedly with triple salary, or suddenly experience devastating failure at work, and yet less than a year later, find that they are about as happy as they were before. Of course, there's a reason for this. From an evolutionary perspective, this characteristic has its roots in humanity's remote past as a species. It is an adaptive feature that helps people survive. Hence, if someone were permanently happy from some success or accomplishment, in a perpetual state of bliss, that would tend to extinguish his or her motivation for the continued development of new skills, growth, and progress. It would kill initiative. Conversely, if someone were naturally inclined to become permanently depressed or discouraged from a failure or loss, it would reduce the odds that he or she would survive, pass down their genes, and become ancestors.

This is why we need balance in life. No matter how satisfying our work, it is a mistake to rely on work as our only source of satisfaction. Just as humans need a varied diet to supply needed vitamins and minerals, so we need a varied diet of activities that can supply a sense of enjoyment and satisfaction. Recognizing that the principle of adaptation is normal, we can anticipate and prepare for it by intentionally cultivating a full range of activities that we enjoy. Some experts suggest that we start by making an inventory of the things we enjoy doing, and if we go through slow periods at work, we can turn to family, friends, hobbies, and other interests as our primary source of satisfaction. And if we shift out interest and attention to other activities for a while, eventually the cycle will swing again, and we can return to our work with renewed interest and enthusiasm.

Job and Career as Calling

Thus far we have identified some of the more common sources of dissatisfaction at work, factors such as boredom, lack of autonomy, and feeling that we are unfairly compensated. When we focus on what factors play the greatest role in influencing our happiness at work, the most important factor is fulfillment from our work. Of course, there can be other factors as well, such as our emotional make-up or the ability to make friends at work, but there is little doubt that our underlying attitude affects our satisfaction and sense of fulfillment at work.

According to a study at New York University, when it comes to underlying attitudes and their influence on the sense of satisfaction at work, workers are generally divided into three categories: those who view work simply as a job, those who view it as a career, and those who view their work as a calling. While the first group is focused primarily on the financial rewards that the work brings, and the second group primarily on advancement, people in the third category tend to love their work, and if they could afford to, they would continue doing the work even if they didn't get paid.

Holistic Work

They see their work as meaningful, as having a higher purpose, and as making a contribution to society or to the world. Those who view their work as a calling tend to have significantly higher work satisfaction and overall life satisfaction than those who view work as a job or career. The idea of calling has to do with the sense of a higher purpose of one's job, as well as possibly also the social good or welfare of others. While it is easier to consider professions such as social work, teaching, and health work as a calling, in all aspects of life, attitude alone can make a big difference in terms of challenge, satisfaction, and in level of engagement with a project, task, or job.

Surprisingly, research reveals that no matter what the particular field or job, a third of the workers see their work as a job, a third as a career, and a third as a calling. Even among nurses, physicians, and social workers, some see work as a job, others as a career, focusing more on promotion and advancement, and others as a calling. Rather than being randomly or arbitrarily selected, these attitudes seem to be based more on the psychological qualities of individuals and their view of their work, instead of on the nature of the work itself.

Always, however, there are individuals who are concerned with achieving excellence in their endeavors, whatever the higher motivation or purpose of their work. Such people want to develop their own personal potential to its highest degree through their work. In such cases, this approach could also be categorized as "calling," particularly if the higher purpose or meaning involves being of help to other people or developing their sense of curiosity and creativity. Again, here one should have proper motivation, and not perform one's work out of strong competition or a sense of jealousy.

Each of us has the capacity to cultivate greater work satisfaction by transforming a job into a calling. No matter what kind of job we have, with some attention and effort we can find greater meaning in our work. In some cases, we might have a boring job, but at the same time may be supporting family, children, or elderly parents. In that case, helping and supporting family could be our higher purpose. In the same way, there are thousands of people who provide the food we eat and the clothes we wear. Individual workers on an assembly line somewhere may not directly see the benefit of their hard labor, but through a little analysis they can realize the indirect benefits to others, be proud of what they do, and have a sense of accomplishment. Workers all over the world are bringing happiness to others, and although on the surface their jobs may appear insignificant, they may realize their jobs cause beneficial effects on people they may never meet.

Others, for instance, may be working for the government or military and consider working for their country as the higher purpose.

Of course, not all people need to work, either due to special financial circumstances or a state of retirement. Under such circumstances, they can enjoy their freedom and the privileges they have. Even then, they can volunteer or act out their role as a good citizen through their attitudes and choices and by participating fully in the choices they have through the democratic process. However, among those who need to work to make a living, it is important they recognize that they are part of their local society as well as members of the larger human society. By actively participating in the workforce, workers are acting as productive members of their society and indirectly making a contribution to the entire society. If people think along these lines, then they can see some purpose in what they do that is beyond simply providing a livelihood or taking care of their needs. That recognition can be enough to give them a sense of purpose or of calling.

This view can be reinforced by simply asking oneself, "What is the alternative to work?" Just hanging around can lead to the danger of drifting into unhealthy habits, such as resorting to drugs, being part of a gang, or acting as a destructive member of society. So, those who are not contributing to their society are likely undermining its stability. If workers think along these lines, they will see a higher purpose to their work.

Happiness and Work

There are few things in life as devastating to people as losing their job. Research studies reveal that unemployment is one of the few facts that cause a significant decrease in life satisfaction. While the concept of unemployment is foreign to many traditional societies, where citizens are mostly farmers, animal herders, or merchants, in modern societies, losing one's job not only affects one's income but also one's self-image. Some individuals make the transition well. They find they are still respected by others and that they still have self-confidence. In the case of retirees, they can perceive retirement as an opportunity to explore new things. So, different people seem to respond to similar circumstances and situations quite differently.

For those who lose their jobs and whose identity is tied to their jobs, it is helpful that they focus on the larger picture. For example, instead of thinking solely about job or income loss, they should widen their self-image by seeing themselves first as human beings with the capacity for

Holistic Work

friendships, kindness, and empathy, and then by realizing that they have roles in addition to those at work, such as being a parent, a child, a brother or sister, or by developing other interests or hobbies. Likewise, when seeking work, or if you are already employed, it is important to keep in mind that human beings are not machines designed solely for production. Human life is more than work, and individuality is central to a full human life, which includes leisure time and spending time with family and friends. If you are looking for work and are able to select your job, choose one that allows the opportunity for creativity as well as for spending time on your hobbies and with your family. Even if it means less pay, it is better to choose work that gives you greater freedom and more time to be with your family or to participate in activities you enjoy.

When I retired from teaching, my wife and I moved to a new town and a small, exclusive neighborhood composed largely of retirees and of people late in their careers. One day, while our next-door neighbor, I heard her mention that for retirees, every day is Saturday. That got me thinking about the common complaint workers make regarding Mondays, and their exclamation at the end of the workweek, "Thank God it's Friday!" If attitude is an important source of happiness, whether at work or in retirement, can't Mondays be Fridays and every day a source of purpose and happiness?

When I first began teaching at Washington & Jefferson College, classes were taught four days a week, and we had something called "Wonderful Wednesday." Unless one was a science major or otherwise enrolled in a lab, Wednesday was a day free from classes. As professor of religious studies and college chaplain, I would often use those days to take students cross-country skiing in the winter and cycling and kayaking the rest of the year. Over the years, I learned to love my profession, and I awoke each day eager to begin my workday teaching classes or counseling students. In addition, I was free to spend the latter part of my afternoons hiking, cycling, or coaching my son's soccer team. I could have chosen a profession that offered higher pay, but I would never have enjoyed the satisfaction I gained as a college professor.

One of the benefits of college teaching and chaplaincy work is counseling and advising students on life choices such as careers and mates. In this regard, I remember hearing President Tori Haring-Smith's advice to freshmen students at the annual opening convocation: "You have come to a liberal arts college to prepare for an average of eight career changes you might make in your lifetime, including preparing for jobs that don't yet exist."

Holistic Happiness

For people able to select the type of work they expect to go into, it is best if they choose work that fits their disposition and temperament. People will certainly be happier and more satisfied if they have an accurate assessment of the demands and expectations of their area of work, as well as self-understanding and awareness of their skills, abilities, and interests. When it comes to family and career, they must be positive and patient in their expectation and adaptable in times of frustration, disappointment, and unemployment, for how people perceive the world is more important to happiness than objective circumstances. Above all, they must acquire and maintain a sense of purpose, in life and play as well as in hardship and work, for there is clearly a correlation between work satisfaction and life satisfaction. When one takes into account all of the variables that affect life satisfaction, including marital status, social supports outside of work, health, faith, and other life circumstances, one can begin to appreciate the tremendous role that work can play in a happy and satisfied life.

In thinking about life's happiest moments, in addition to events associated with marriage or children, often we think of work-related events, particularly beginnings and endings, or, as they used to be called, rites of passage. In my case, I think of the occasion of my ordination to ministry, or the day I passed my oral exam for my master's degree and the process of successfully defending a dissertation for my PhD, which prepared me to experience additional times of happiness, such as the publication of my first book and landing teaching jobs at Grove City College and at Washington & Jefferson College. In addition to satisfaction gained from a forty-year teaching career, I also recall with joy the day of my retirement from full-time teaching. Nevertheless, I'm not sure I ever transitioned successfully into the ranks of retirement, for I find great satisfaction in work, particularly in research, teaching, and writing. Having published some fifteen books thus far in my retirement years, I have learned from my wife that I have failed at retirement, the one failure I embrace.

Questions for Discussion and Reflection

In addition to the questions listed at the end of the preface, answer the following questions, writing your answers in a journal. If you are in a group study, be prepared to share your answers with those in the group.

Holistic Work

1. If you could improve work conditions, where would you start, with a change in your boss, with your co-workers, or with your work environment? Explain your answer.

2. If you were able to maintain your job during the recent pandemic, how did stress, fear, and concerns for safety and security affect your workplace? What did you, your co-workers, or your superiors do to improve conditions? What did you, your co-workers, or your superiors do to make conditions worse? In retrospect, how could things have been done differently during the pandemic, both at home, at work, or by government and society?

3. Have you witnessed situations at work where one person made a significant impact, positively or negatively, on morale or job satisfaction? If so, explain your answer.

4. Have you witnessed situations at work that illustrate the author's point that the workplace can provide opportunities to cultivate values such as compassion, patience, tolerance, and forgiveness? Explain your answer.

5. On a scale of 1 to 10, with 10 being the highest, where would you rank money or pay as a means of job satisfaction? Where would you rank happiness; challenge; and co-workers?

6. Have you ever experienced the state of "flow" at work? If so, describe your experience.

7. While pleasure may not fully define happiness, the two conditions are clearly related, aren't they? Explain your answer.

8. Explain and assess the role of adaptation in job satisfaction.

9. Do you agree with the author's position that viewing one's work as calling, rather than simply as a job or career, can positively affect workplace happiness and satisfaction? Explain your answer.

10. If you are retired from work or are contemplating retirement, what joys and fears do you find associated with that decision or state? Explain your answer.

11. In your estimation, what is the single-most important factor in work satisfaction" In life happiness?

8

Holistic Consuming

AT THIS POINT IN human history, we have enough material resources to feed, clothe, shelter, and educate every living individual on earth. Not only that, we have the global capacity to enhance health care, fight major diseases, and considerably clean up the environment. Nonetheless, a quick examination at this warming globe tells us just how far we are from achieving any of these goals. In the past several centuries, the human community has divided into two distinct worlds: a "first" world filled with opulence, luxury, and material excess, and a "third" world characterized by deprivation, poverty, and struggle. Whereas first and third worlds could formerly be distinguished along national boundaries, increasingly one finds pockets of wealth surrounded by ever widening regions of impoverishment. Most of the world's population is now growing up in winner-take-all economies, where the main goal of individuals is to get whatever they can for themselves. Within this economic landscape, selfishness and materialism are being seen as goals of life.[1]

This global reality exists, however, only because each one of us readily converted to the ideology of consumerism and materialism. Indeed, mass conversion seems already to have occurred. Vast numbers of us are coming to accept the idea that to be well, we first have to be well off. And many of us, unfortunately, are learning to evaluate our identity in terms of our own well-being and accomplishment, not by looking inward at our spirit or integrity, but by looking outward at what we have and what we can buy. Similarly, we have adopted a worldview in which the worth and success of

1. Richard Ryan's "Foreword" to Kasser, *High Price of Materialism*, ix.

others is judged not by their apparent wisdom, kindness, or community contributions, but in terms of whether they possess the right clothes, the right car, and more generally, the right "stuff."

Perhaps the most insidious aspect of this modern measure of worth is that it is not simply about having enough, but about having more than others do. That is, feelings of personal worth are based on how one's financial resources and possessions compares with that of others. Accordingly, at all levels of wealth one can find individuals who crave gadgets that are ever more expensive, status symbols, and image builders, and who subjectively feel that they need more than they currently have. As advertising executives have known for decades, people become good consumers only when they convert mere "desires" into urgent "needs." By this criterion, most of us have become good consumers.[2]

Are the promises of consumer society true or false? Social institutions, it seems, cannot agree. Wherever we turn, we receive conflicting answers. We can ask the government, but while politicians worry that popular consumer culture has displaced community and family values, economic considerations play a key role in the decisions of most elected officials. We can turn to religious leaders, but while the Bible says that a person who cares about wealth will have trouble entering the kingdom of heaven, some churches, many of them large and new, are pulling in millions of dollars, often to promote elaborate building campaigns and meet the needs of expanding programs and staff.

If we turn to psychology for answers, we find a similar ambivalence about materialistic values. One the one hand, much of the work conducted by evolutionary and behavioral psychologists is compatible with the notion that attainment of wealth and status is of great importance. Similarly, behavioral theories such as those of B. F. Skinner hold that the successful attainment of external rewards is a motivator of all behavior, and indeed fundamental to individuals' adaptation to society. The behaviorist idea that happiness and satisfaction come from attaining wealth and possessions is exemplified by the fact that the founder of American behaviorism, John Watson, took the basic psychological principles of learning and applied them to advertising on Madison Avenue, a model followed by many psychologists.

While behavioral and evolutionary theories largely dominated American academic psychology in the last century, humanistic and existential thinkers such as Carl Rogers, Abraham Maslow, and Erich Fromm voiced

---

2. Richard Ryan's "Foreword" to Kasser, *High Price of Materialism*, x.

Holistic Happiness

a sharply contrasting opinion about materialistic pursuits. Although they acknowledged that some level of material comfort is necessary to provide for basic physical needs, these psychologists suggested that materialistic values can detract from well-being and happiness. Humanistic and existential psychologists place qualities such as authentic self-expression, intimate relationships, and contribution to the community at the core of their notions of psychological health. From this perspective, "a strong focus on materialistic pursuits not only distracts people from experiences conducive to psychological growth and health, but also signals a fundamental alienation from what is truly meaningful."[3]

What does research show? Does money buy happiness? Does affluence make us healthier and better adjusted psychologically? What happens to the quality of our lives when we value materialism?

It would be one thing if the promises of the consumer society were real, but they are not. The formidable body of research into consumerism indicates a surprising and quite counter-intuitive fact, that even when people obtain more money and material goods, they do not become more satisfied with their lives, or more psychologically healthy as a result. More specifically, once people are above the poverty levels of income, gains in wealth have little to no payoff in terms of happiness or well-being. In addition, according to the research results that Tim Kasser reports in his 2002 *The High Price of Materialism*, merely aspiring to have greater wealth or more material possessions is likely to be associated with increased personal unhappiness. The American dream, it seems, has a dark side, and the pursuit of wealth and possessions might actually be undermining our well-being.[4]

As Kasser shows, people with strong materialistic values and desires report more symptoms of anxiety, are at greater risk for depression, low self-esteem, and problems of intimacy, and experience more frequent physical discomfort than those who are less materialistic. They watch more television, use more alcohol and drugs, and have more impoverished personal relationships. Even in sleep, their dreams seem to be infected with anxiety and distress. And these results are the same for all individuals, regardless of age, income, or culture.

In case one thinks these results only apply to North Americans, it is interesting to note that similar correlations between materialistic values and increased feelings of anger, anxiety, and depression, namely, decreased

---

3. Kasser, *High Price of Materialism*, 2.
4. Kasser, *High Price of Materialism*, 9.

life satisfaction, have been replicated in samples from around the world, including in England, Denmark, Germany, India, Romania, Russia, South Korea, China, Turkey, Australia, and Singapore.[5]

Another element that these studies measure is narcissistic tendencies. In psychological terms, narcissism describes people who cover an inner feeling of emptiness and questionable self-worth with a grandiose exterior that brags of self-importance. Narcissists are typically vain, expect special treatment from others, and can be manipulative and hostile toward others. Social critics and psychologists often suggest that consumer culture breeds a narcissistic personality by glorifying consumption (for example, "Have it your way," or "You can have it all!").

Recent studies also examine the extent to which materialism is associated with the use of substances such as tobacco, alcohol, and drugs. One study of college students asked how many cigarettes they smoked on a typical day, how often they chewed tobacco, and how often in the last year they had gotten drunk, smoked marijuana, and done hard drugs. When those five indicators were averaged, results showed that young adults with a strong materialistic value orientation are highly likely to use such substances frequently. Unfortunately, these results are confirmed in studies of high school students. Materialistic teens are more likely to engage in these risk behaviors than are teens focused on other values. In samples of adolescents, college students, and adults, with various means of measuring materialistic values and well-being, results show that the more materialistic values people have, the more their quality of life is diminished. Specifically, these studies show that materialistic values are associated with low self-actualization and well-being, as well as more antisocial behavior and narcissism.

Kasser highlights two reasons why materialism is associated with unhappiness. The first concerns the burdens that materialism places on the human spirit. Desire to have increasingly more material goods drive consumers into an ever more frantic pace of life. Not only must they work harder, but, once possessing goods, they have to maintain, upgrade, replace, insure, and constantly manage them. Rather than controlling possessions, they control us. Thus, in the journey of life, materialists end up carrying an ever-heavier load, one that expends the energy necessary for living, loving, and learning—the really satisfying aspects of that journey. Thus materialism, although promising happiness, actually creates dissatisfaction and psychological strain.

5. Kasser, *High Price of Materialism*, 21–22.

Holistic Happiness

The second explanation is surprising. If materialism causes unhappiness, unhappiness also "causes" materialism. Enhanced desires or "needs" to consume more are actually deeply connected with feelings of personal insecurity. Materialism, it appears, tends to thrive among people who feel uncertain about matters of love, self-esteem competence, or control. Indeed, to many people materialism appears to offer a solution to these common insecurities and anxieties. Our consumer culture persistently teaches that we can counter unhappiness or insecurity by buying our way to self-esteem and loveworthiness. That's the pervasive message passed on in popular media, that we will feel better about ourselves if we are surrounded by symbols of worth—gadgets that others admire, clothes and adornments that convey attractiveness, or image products that communicate vitality and self-importance. As research indicates, it is because our psychological insecurities are so easily connected with the promise of self-esteem that we keep on consuming.[6]

Remarkably, then, economies focused on consumption appear, in turn, to foster conditions that heighten psychological insecurities, and in this sense they fuel themselves. Children grow up in homes where their parents crave products and possessions. Parents today work more hours outside the home than ever, many to acquire the buying power to obtain more of the goods they have been taught they and their children "need." Meantime, attention to children, intimate time with spouses, and other relationships get pushed to the periphery. Not much for living remains after the working, shopping, and consuming are completed. Yet during this free time, children and adults occupy themselves with mass media crammed with advertisements that entice and promise good feelings ahead. Thus, the cultural climate of consumerism creates the very circumstance where love, control, and esteem are not securely experienced, and in which ever-present self-scrutiny is fostered. In this climate, almost everyone is vulnerable.

If, as evidence show, people strongly oriented to materialistic values are at risk for addiction because they experience low well-being, why is this so? Do materialistic values cause people's problems, or is it the case that people who are already unhappy focus on wealth, possessions, image, and popularity? The answers to these questions are clearly complicated, but they begin with the idea of psychological needs.

Although no one disagrees that all people have certain physical needs (e.g., air, water, food, and shelter) that must be met to ensure survival, some

---

6. Kasser, *High Price of Materialism*, 28, 52.

social scientists stop there, saying that psychological needs are either impossible to prove scientifically or do not exist. Some theorists, however, apply the concept of psychological needs to understand human motivation and well-being, and they are supported by substantial research, which suggests that people are highly motivated to feel safe and secure, competent, connected to others, and autonomous and authentically engaged in their behavior. Well-being and quality of life increase when these four sets of needs are satisfied, and decrease when they are not. Materialistic values become prominent in the lives of many individuals who have a history of not having their needs well met. However, materialistic values are not just expressions of unhappiness. Instead, they lead people to organize their lives in ways that do a poor job of satisfying their needs, and thus contribute even more to people's misery.

The family is the primary socializing environment for most of our early years, and the experiences we have there strongly determine the extent to which we feel safe and secure. The ways parents treat their children, the stability of the family, and the socioeconomic circumstances in which children are raised have important influence in terms of fulfilling needs for safety, sustenance, and security. When family environments poorly satisfy these needs, many children respond by adopting values that emphasize wealth and possessions. Additionally, when mothers are warm, affectionate, and appreciative of their children, whether they impose many rules and strictures on their children, and how much they allow their children to express their own opinions and be their own person, also influence whether teenagers strongly value financial success or place more value on self-acceptance, good relationships, or contribute to the community.

While people might assume that greater wealth is associated with greater materialism, studies indicate that teenagers who strongly value materialism are more likely to come from poorer socioeconomic backgrounds than are children who value self-acceptance, relationships, and community contributions. If growing up in poverty and poor neighborhoods may be partly responsible for creating a materialistic value orientation, this may be due to the fact that such social environments often lead children to feel unsafe and insecure. Unmet needs, then, rather than preexistent wealth, are strong determinants in driving youth to value the materialistic pursuits encouraged by society. Thus, materialistic values can be both a symptom of an underlying insecurity and a coping strategy taken on in an attempt to alleviate problems and satisfy needs.

Holistic Happiness

The problem is that materialistic values are rather poor coping strategies. As with other coping strategies that may make people feel good in the short term (self-isolation, denial of a problem, hedonistic pleasures such as drinking, drugs, and sex), materialistic pursuits may in the long term actually maintain and deepen feelings of insecurity. Negative associations between materialistic values and well-being certainly suggest that such a coping strategy is not especially useful in alleviating people's problems. In fact, it probably makes problems worse.

While people generally believe that getting what they want makes them feel good about themselves and their life, evidence suggests that beyond having enough money to meet basic needs, attaining wealth, possessions, and status does not yield long-term increases in happiness or well-being. Even the successful pursuit of materialistic ideals typically turns out to be empty and unsatisfying. Even though Americans earn twice as much in today's dollars as they did in 1957, for example, the proportion of those telling surveyors that they are "very happy" has declined from 35 to 29 percent. Even very rich people report being only slightly happier than average Americans are. Indeed, in most nations the correlation between income and happiness is negligible. Only in the poorest countries, such as Bangladesh and India, is income a measure of emotional well-being.[7]

Self-esteem is understood by most psychologists to be based on people's evaluations of themselves. When people have high self-esteem, they have more positive than negative self-evaluations, feeling good about themselves, and believing they are worthy and valuable. In contrast, people with low self-esteem have more negative than positive evaluations about themselves, felling unworthy, unloved, and inadequate. Many studies have been conducted to understand the role of self-esteem in people's lives, In brief, high self-esteem comes in part from growing up in a warm environment with loving parents and from successfully using one's competencies and abilities to attain one's goals. Low self-esteem occurs when people are neglected and belittled, and when they feel unable to get what they want. This fragile, unstable self-esteem is called "contingent."

Contingent self-esteem clearly shares much in common with how materialistic values are conceived. Values for money, image, and fame cluster together because they all focus on extrinsic concerns. Thus, people with materialistic values hinge their self-esteem and self-worth on whether

---

7. This information, reported by psychologists David Myers and Ed Diener, is cited in Kasser, *High Price of Materialism*, 3.

they have attained some reward (money) or whether other people praise them. Contingent self-esteem is also prominent in one of the psychological problems that occurs with materialistic values, namely, narcissism. Many social critics claim that narcissism is the disorder of our materialistic society, and some theorist note that it often develops as a defense against low self-esteem. According to such views, narcissists attempt to cover feelings of inadequacy by going to the opposite extreme, hiding behind a false sense of worth that is typically dependent on external accomplishments.

Another way in which materialistic individuals may have difficulty in fulfilling their needs for esteem and competence derives from discrepancies. Many psychologists believe that people's emotional states are largely a function of how far they are from where they ideally would like to be. Discrepancies can apply to almost any aspect of people's lives, including their bodies, personalities, and relationships. One person might want straight hair even though hers is curly; another man wishes he were more outgoing instead of shy; another wishes she were younger looking; while another wishes he had more hair. Discrepancies can motivate people to engage in beneficial behavior, but if the discrepancy is chronic, or if people feel unable to resolve it, needs for esteem and competence can remain unfulfilled.

While it is natural for people to want to improve their skills, appearance, personality, and intelligence, it is unnatural to pursue these aims obsessively or fanatically, whether through compulsive exercise, cosmetic overuse, sexual enhancements, or recurring liposuction and facelift treatments. While self-improvement is good, perfectionism is not. Ultimately, self-acceptance is essential to happiness, and aging normally and graciously more attractive and healthier than succumbing to Hollywood and Wall Street standards of beauty, success, and well-being.

The ideals that people strive for, and that partly determine discrepancies, come from a number of sources. Personal values are one obvious source, as are societal standards in general. People also develop ideals by looking at the lives of their friends, neighbors, co-workers, and relatives. A great deal of information about what is ideal comes from our culture, particularly through educational, religious, and political systems.

For people oriented toward materialistic values, however, each of these sources can lead to the formation of ideals concerning money, possessions, looks, and status. Several lines of research suggest, however, that these ideals frequently increase one's discrepancies, and thus one's dissatisfaction. And when materialistic ideals romanticize wealth and possessions, to the extent that ideals become unreachable, chronic discrepancies are likely to result. In addition, even if one can reach such ideals, it is not likely to improve one's quality of life. As a result, people may form even higher materialistic ideals, creating new discrepancies and further dissatisfaction. People with strong materialistic orientations are likely to watch a great deal of television, comparing themselves unfavorably with personalities they see there, thereby lowering life satisfaction.

As data show, pursuing materialistic goals, even doing so successfully, fails to increase personal happiness. People may experience temporary improvement of mood, but it is likely to be short-lived and superficial. The sad truth is that when people feel the emptiness of either material success or failure, they often persist in thinking that more will be better, and thus continue to strive for what will never make them happier. In the process, they fail to correct the underlying psychological issues that led them to such an empty pursuit in the first place, and ignore important psychological needs, such as improving interpersonal relationships and becoming involved in one's community, two cornerstones of personal well-being.

Because values have broad effects on human behavior, the extent to which individuals focus on materialistic pursuits affects the way they interact with other people. When people place strong emphasis on consuming and buying, earning and spending, and focusing regularly on the monetary worth of things, they likely will treat people like things. Philosopher Martin Buber referred to this interpersonal stance as I-It relationships, in which others' qualities, subjective experience, feelings, and desires are ignored, seen as unimportant, or are viewed only in terms of their usefulness to oneself. In such relationships, other people become reduced to objects, little different from products that may be purchased, used, and discarded. Buber contrasted this objectifying type of relationship with an I-Thou relationship in which other people are recognized as valuable entities in themselves, different from oneself but just as important.[8]

Thus far we have examined three ways in which materialistic values detract from well-being: they maintain deep-rooted feelings of insecurity, they lead to fruitless and never-ending attempts to prove competence, and they interfere with relationships. There is another way in which materialistic values work against need satisfaction and psychological health: they diminish personal freedom. Stated differently, a strong focus on the pursuit of wealth, fame, and image undermines the satisfaction of needs for authenticity and autonomy.

---

8. Kasser, *High Price of Materialism*, 67.

Holistic Consuming

At first, this too seems counterintuitive, for we consider freedom and capitalism to go hand in hand, and consumer goods and personal appearance as primary means by which we express our individual identities. Studies show that individuals who are strongly oriented toward materialistic values place little emphasis on valuing connectedness to others and to their community. A similar value conflict is evident between materialism and autonomy. To the extent that people value wealth, fame, and image, they correspondingly place less value on authenticity and therefore on freedom.

Materialistic values are associated with placing little value on freedom and self-direction, thereby decreasing the likelihood of satisfying these needs. Individuals strongly concerned with materialistic values also enter experiences already focused on obtaining rewards and praise, rather than on enjoying the challenges and inherent pleasures of activities. Furthermore, their values direct them toward activities such as watching television and shopping that rarely provide flow or intrinsic motivation. Finally, materialistic values are associated with the tendency to feel pressured and compelled, even in behaviors consistent with these values. Pressure, control, and compulsion, rather than providing paths to freedom and autonomy, make people feel chained and imprisoned. Subtle societal impulses such as these—demeaning, destructive, and addictive—define a life focused on materialistic values.

The struggle against materialism and consumerism rages. Its effects may not be as obvious as the war against opioids and other harmful narcotics, but the results are equally devastating: the loss of soul. The starting point in our battle against rampant consumerism and marketeering is none other than raised consciousness concerning who we are, what we value, and what we strive for in this worldly existence.

When I think of the unhappiness and suffering caused by unhealthy consumption, I am reminded of the Four Noble Truths of Buddhism, which underscore the correlation between suffering and wrong or immoderate desire. What we consume can be the cause of much of our suffering. The Buddha spoke of Four Nutriments, of four kinds of food that can bring either well-being or ill-being. According to the Buddha, if people look deeply into their consumptive patterns and identify the nature of the nutrients that have shaped them, they are already on the path of transformation and healing.

The first kind of nutriment is edible food, what we actually put into our mouths, chew, swallow, or drink. If it is good food, healthy food in moderation, the result is well-being. If it is not healthy, appropriate, or in

Holistic Happiness

moderation, then we can become ill or unhealthy. Mindful consumption of edible food also affects how we shop. Mindful shopping means we know what to buy and what not to buy. Mindful consumption also affects the way we cook. When we cook, we have another occasion to be aware and practice mindfulness, not only of our own need for health, but also of how we can reduce the suffering of others. Merely by the way we shop, cook, and eat, we can help preserve our planet.

The second kind of nutriment is sensory impressions. This kind of food is not consumed with our mouths, but with our minds and senses. Depending on the content, consuming television, news, books, films, the Internet, and conversation can be either healthy or toxic. Sometime we try to escape suffering with even more consumption, which brings additional suffering. We are upset, and so we watch additional television shows or binge on video games or social media, and then, depending on the experience, we can feel even more upset. Sensory consumption also includes what we hear from others. If we listen to gossip, judgment, insult, or bias, then we are consuming these things. If what we consume fills us with anger, irritation, or craving, then it adds to the overall irritation, violence, and suffering in the world. In such situations, it is useful to develop a strategy of mindful consumption so that what we read, watch, and listen to doesn't elevate our distress and that of others.

The third kind of nutriment is volition, also called aspiration or desire. Each of us has deep desire within, and this provides us with passion and motivation. This desire can be healthy or toxic and can cause well-being or suffering. When the Buddha left his palace to become a monk, he wished to be enlightened in order to overcome willful obstacles and succeed in his desire to alleviate global suffering. Compassion is a positive energy, but there are other kinds of desires, like the desire to hurt others or for revenge, which are toxic. Each of us needs to look within and identify our deepest desire, whether it is healthy or not, and whether it is bringing us suffering or happiness, because that is food that nourishes our lives.

The fourth kind of nutriment is consciousness. We are influenced by the ways of thinking of people around us, and we consume the views of others in many ways. Individual consciousness is affected by collective consciousness, and collective consciousness is affected by individual consciousness. It is consciousness that shapes our social world, determining our happiness or unhappiness. If we live in an environment where people are angry and violent, then sooner or later we will become angry and cruel.

Holistic Consuming

Conversely, if we live in an environment where people are joyous, compassionate, and optimistic, sooner or later we will become generous, compassionate, and happy.

The Buddha viewed happiness as being inherent in the human spirit, and of suffering as coming primarily from our minds and how we see the world. In this respect, the Buddhist tradition speaks of *samyojana*, ten knots or fetters that bind and deprive us of our freedom. The first fetter is craving. The danger of craving is that we believe that the object of our craving is what we really want, and that it is what can truly bring us happiness. However, when craving arises in us, we are no longer at peace. We are no longer satisfied with what we have and who we are. Craving is like a hook and bait we use to catch fish. When the fish sees the bait, it looks appealing; but the fish doesn't know that inside the bait there is a hook. The object of our craving is like that bait. It looks appealing and the fish bites it and gets hooked. When we look mindfully at the object of our craving, often it loses its appeal and we are able to avoid the hidden dangers of the objects of our craving.

The second fetter is anger and violence. The flame of anger is as destructive as the flame of craving. When anger overcomes us, we have no peace and no capacity to be happy. However, if we understand the nature and causes of suffering, we will see that our anger often arises from ignorance and wrong views. If we feel anger arising in us, we can take a step back and practice breathing in such a way that we can untie the knot of our anger.

The third fetter is ignorance, or what Buddhists call wrong view. Often we are confused and don't know where to turn or what to do. So from our ignorance, we say and do the wrong things; instead of sitting with our ignorance and letting wisdom and discernment arise, we act out of ignorance. That is the third kind of knot we must unravel.

The fourth fetter is our complexes that cause us to spend our time and energy comparing ourselves to others. There are three complexes: superiority, inferiority, and equality. Each of these binds us, even the equality complex, because we focus on a sense of self versus others, and we find ourselves competing with others. These complexes exist because we have the notion that we are a separate self. This notion is the origin of the three complexes, and they only bring suffering.

The fifth fetter is doubt and suspicion. When these are allowed to fester within, we are not at peace. Our suspicion and doubt may come from our ignorance, complexes, or our craving. Perhaps we know what is right, but our suspicions and doubts keep us from acting on it.

Holistic Happiness

The sixth through the tenth fetters focus on the wrong perceptions and wrong views that lead to our suffering. The sixth fetter is the view that my body is my true self, and that my separate self is my actual self. The seventh fetter is dualism, the belief that opposites are unrelated. To be caught in duality—such as that birth and death are opposites, or sameness and otherness, inside or outside, and being and nonbeing—is to have wrong view. The Middle Way of Buddhism, midway between life's extremes, is the way of nonduality. It transcends all pairs of opposites, including being and nonbeing, right and wrong, birth and death, inside and outside, and object and subject. When we learn about something, we usually form an opinion about it. But if we are driven by that opinion, and close ourselves off from further information or ideas that change that opinion, we cannot progress spiritually. So whatever we have learned or heard or been taught, we must be careful not to conder it to be the absolute truth. We should be able to let it go in order to arrive at a higher truth.

The eighth fetter is attachment to views, and Buddhism encourages nonattachment to views. The ninth fetter is similar, only in this case it is attachment to wrong views and perceptions. The tenth fetter is attachment to rites and rituals as paths to salvation or means of liberation. Actually, there is no one belief, action, thought, or ritual that brings salvation, enlightenment, or liberation. The path to liberation is better described as "letting go," as nonattachment to wrong perception, wrong thinking, wrong speech, and wrong action. Liberation requires continual practice, continual commitment to mindfulness, concentration, and insight, and continual letting go of cherished beliefs and views. Only then can we move to well-being and the transformation of suffering. When the roots of suffering are absent, we can be free and happy, and we can act ethically, motivated by our awareness and compassion.

The journey of spirituality begins with the realization that it is possible to live happily in the present moment. Imagine you are a child walking by a bakery. You see many delicious items inside and the aroma is enticing. Imagine the owner inviting you in and saying, "You can have whatever you want. The whole shop is for you." How would you react? And where would you begin?

When we come home to the present moment, filled with innumerable wonderful things and so many opportunities for happiness, we may feel like that child. How do we respond? And where do we begin? This is the opportunity we all face, and the key to success is simplicity. We can begin with

Holistic Consuming

mindfulness—mindful breathing, thinking, and action—and see whether we can handle the beauty and happiness that life offers. It is important that we cultivate our capacity for happiness, realizing that happiness is only available in the present.

When we are mindful of something, we naturally concentrate on it. If we hold a delicious ice cream cone, and concentrate on that cone, mindfulness enhances both the flavor and the experience. Our focus is not on the past, the future, or lost on other projects. The cone is the object of our concentration, and in that moment we are happy. When we are mindful of something, we naturally concentrate on it; when we are mindful and concentrated, insight arises. Insight makes us happy, because insight is liberating. If we are fearful, we cannot be joyful or content. If we worry, we can't be peaceful or happy. But when we have insight, fear and worry are removed and true happiness is possible.

Looking superficially, we might be annoyed when it rains or snows. But when we understand deeply, we perceive that rain and snow are wonderful, renewing and refreshing the earth year round. Looking deeply—mindfully, simply—enables us to enjoy all things, and life becomes enjoyable. Buddhists have a word for this condition, *samtusta*, which means that we have enough in our lives to make us happy, that what we have is sufficient.[9] *Samtusta* can also be translated as "the awareness that one is satisfied with little." When one is aware of the conditions of happiness already present in one's life, one usually finds that they are more than enough for present happiness.

We all know people without a big house or a new car who are content with what they have. We also know people who have plenty of money, power, and success who are deeply unhappy. We can't receive wellbeing and happiness from others. Each of us must walk the path for ourselves, practicing living happily in the present. *Samtusta*—non-craving—may be difficult to understand at first, but if we observe what we see in and around us, it becomes clear. We can choose to focus our awareness on beautiful sights, listen deeply to those who use thoughtful speech, and make a concentrated effort to embrace the gift of simplicity. Furthermore, each of us has the capacity not only for happiness, but also for bringing happiness to others. If humans are able to walk on this path together, it will be on account of our practice of *samtusta*, not on account of a rule of law or because of a divine commandment.

---

9. The discussion on *samtusta* is adapted from Hanh, *Good Citizens*, 58–60.

Some eight hundred years ago Francis of Assisi noted that what we own owns us. Those who have possessions are owned by their possessions. This seems unavoidable, particularly to those who place little value or fail to give voice to their soul. The true goal of all religions is to lead us back to the place where everything is one, to the experience of radical unity with humanity, nature, and with God. Religion has no other purpose than to make possible this one journey. Such a journey is difficult to describe with words, for the crucial point is that it's my personal journey and your personal journey, a journey one must take individually.

Simplicity need not be defined in the negative—as a life free of craving, as self-denial, or even as sacrifice. Simplicity, properly understood, fills us with joy and happiness. According to the teachings of Buddhism, simplifying our lives allows us to look deeply into things. When we do, we discover the interdependence and impermanence of all things, the source of compassion.

Authentic spirituality reminds us that ill-being can be transformed. There is a path that leads to happiness, and it begins with the understanding that each of us is made in the image of God, or as Buddhism teaches, that each of us has the Buddha nature inside. We all have the ability to be mindful, to be focused, to have wisdom and insight, and to be wholly compassionate. Aware of the suffering caused by unmindful consumption, Buddhist teaching on the Four Kinds of Nutriments can help us overcome the regrets and sorrows that drag us back into the past, or the anxieties, fear, or cravings that thwart us from living fully in the present moment. To live fully, let us determine not to cover up loneliness, anxiety, or other suffering by losing ourselves in consumption. Rather, let us consume in ways that preserve peace, joy, and well-being in our body and consciousness and in the collective body and consciousness of our family, our society, and our earth.

Questions for Discussion and Reflection

In addition to the questions listed at the end of the preface, answer the following questions, writing your answers in a journal. If you are in a group study, be prepared to share your answers with those in the group.

1. Assess the concepts of consumption and wealth as a measure of worth in society.

Holistic Consuming

2. Do you agree or disagree with behaviorist psychologist such as B. F. Skinner and John Watson that happiness and satisfaction come from attaining wealth and possessions? Explain your answer.

3. Do you agree or disagree with humanist psychologists such as Carl Rogers, Abraham Maslow, and Erich Fromm that materialistic values can detract from well-being and happiness? Explain your answer.

4. Are materialism and selfishness connected? Are they "joined at the hip," or merely tangentially related? Explain your answer.

5. After reading this chapter, what did you learn about the connection between consumerism and narcissism?

6. After reading this chapter, what did you learn about the connection between the conditions of one's home or upbringing and addictive behavior?

7. After reading this chapter, what did you learn about the connection between self-esteem and materialistic values?

8. What is your idea of the "good life"? How much is sufficient and how do we know when we have enough material belongings and adequate economic security?

9. How are politics, religion, and psychology ambivalent about materialistic values?

10. What critique should we make of our consumer culture?

11. Assess Tim Kasser's conclusions that connect materialistic values with personal unhappiness and decreased life satisfaction.

12. After reading this chapter, what did you learn about the Four Nutriments. What did you learn about their correlation with well-being or ill-being?

13. After reading this chapter, what did the concept of *samyojana* teach you about the correlation between consumption, happiness, and well-being?

9

Holistic Eating and Exercise

BY ENCOURAGING US TO be all we are and can be, spirituality connects us with the divine, both internally and externally, thereby offering us the full resources of the universe. In this regard, good health and well-being are available to all who seek and ask, particularly to those who eat healthily and exercise regularly. We can extend the quality of our everyday lives and our bodily healthy by eating well, remaining active, taking time for ourselves, and managing stress. Working to make the second half of life physically, emotionally, and spiritually healthier than the first can pay enormous dividends. The material in this chapter is intended to provide you with information you need to live a happier and healthier life for years to come.

The Sacrament of the Present Moment

Nutrition is an important aspect of consumption, and how we eat, whether too much, not enough, or just right, is often an effective indicator of compulsive or restrained desire. As we all know, the saying, "We are what we eat," is only partially true. More significant, however, is how we eat and why we eat as we do.

A basic principle in eating holistically is to consider eating from a sacramental point of view. Since the concept of a sacrament is part of Christian theology, let us take a moment to speak of sacramental theology, for not all Christians agree on the meaning of a sacrament, or even on its value. While Roman Catholic and Eastern Orthodox Christians recognize seven sacraments, most Protestants only recognize two, while Protestants such as

Quakers, the Salvation Army, and Adventist groups discount their use and value, and most Baptists prefer the term "ordinances."

The word sacrament is derived from a Latin phrase that means "to make holy." As commonly affirmed, a sacrament is a visible means of divine grace. Underlying the term "sacrament" is the realization that God's presence can be experienced in the ordinary and the natural, and that visible and tactile objects can serve as doorways to divinity. This is why each of the formal sacraments of the church insist on a material element such as bread, wine, and water. Rather than eliminating the concept altogether, as some Protestants do, or limiting sacraments to two, as most Protestants do, I favor the inclusive approach taken by Catholic and Orthodox Christians, which includes the laying on of hands and the physicality of marriage itself.

However, if we understand the basic principle underlying sacramental theology, we will come to experience the grace of the risen Christ in all natural settings. As the author of John's gospel states in the remarkable prefatory passage known as the Logos Hymn, all things came into being through Christ, and as a result, all living things are life producing, for all are grounded in the Logos becoming flesh (John 1:1–4, 14). The core message of the incarnation of the Logos in Jesus is that the divine presence is here, in us and in all of creation. The sacramental principle is this: Begin with a concrete moment of encounter, based in the physical world, and the divine Spirit universalizes from these, so that what is true in heaven becomes true on earth. Thus, the spiritual journey proceeds with ever-greater circles of inclusion, beginning with what theologians wisely call the "scandal of the particular." The purest form of spirituality is to find God here and now, and to experience what the French mystic Jean Pierre de Caussade (1675–1751) called "the sacrament of the present moment."

When Jesus spoke the words "This is my body," I believe he was speaking not only about the bread in front of him, but about the whole universe, about everything that is physical, natural, and yet spirit-filled. Thus understood, the sacrament of the Eucharist is not exclusive to specific elements or administered only by ordained clergy, but is a possibility latent in all things.

When we see through this expansive lens, we discover that the more we cultivate intimacy with the natural world, the more we discover about God's presence. All our interactions with nature can be sacramental, and all the ways nature extends to us are sacramental as well. This discovery that every creature and every created thing can be a window of revelation into the divine nature is an invitation to fall more in love with nature, and to surround our ways of life with reverence and grace. Sacramental vision means not only that we grow in our love of Gd's ways in the world, but also that we grow in our sense of kinship with nature. This sense of God's incarnate presence in creation makes our senses shimmer when we walk out in the world aware of its sacramental nature.

In this regard, the bread and wine of the Eucharist are stand-ins for the very elements of the universe, which also enjoy and communicate the incarnate presence. Rather than displaying an exclusive presence, the sacraments communicate a truly inclusive presence. When believers partake of the bread and cup, they are actually affirming the universe as the body of God. In speaking of the Eucharist, Jesus did not say "Think about this" or even "Sacralize this alone." Instead he said, "Eat this!" We must keep eating and drinking this mystery until it dawns on us, "My God, we truly are what we eat! We truly are the body of Christ!" The bottom line in sacramental theology is this: We are not simply human beings having a God experience; rather, in some mysterious way, we are God having a human experience! If we sacralize divinity in natural elements, we end up sacralizing the same divinity in ourselves.

Holistic Eating

Viewing eating from a sacramental point of view grants us freedom but also responsibility. Each of us has a unique physique, metabolism, and appetite. Encompassing these qualities is the Aristotelian proviso of moderation or "the mean." In terms of eating, what this means is that what is sufficient or appropriate for one person may not be adequate for another, and what one person considers wholesome, nutritious, and edible may not suit another. Only you can decide how to eat sacramentally. To do so mindfully, I suggest that you pray for wisdom, guidance, and discernment, while always remaining teachable and willing to adapt and change when necessary. As you do, do not forget that quantities and foods that were once adequate and healthy may not be so today or tomorrow.

Whether or not you eat sacramentally, remember to eat lots of fruit, vegetables, and whole grains, in addition to a variety of protein such as seafood, lean meats, and poultry, in addition to eggs, legumes, soy products, low-fat yogurt, and nuts and seeds. To stay within your daily calorie needs, avoid overeating. If your favorite recipes call for fried fish or breaded chicken, try healthier variations by baking or grilling.

Holistic Eating and Exercise

To obtain the nutrients and other substances needed for good health, vary the foods that you eat. Healthy eating is about balance. You can enjoy your favorite comfort foods, even if they are high in calories, fat, or added sugars. The key is eating them less often and in smaller quantities, and balancing them with healthier foods and increased physical activity. Remember to avoid highly processed foods, added sugars, baked sweets, salty snacks, sweetened drinks, and alcoholic beverages.

Foods such as wheat and dairy products contain allergens. If you get an upset stomach after eating dairy or gluten, by all means avoid them. However, this does not mean they are bad for everyone. As a rule of thumb, keep the following principle in mind: "There is no good food or bad food. Rather, there is a balanced diet and an unbalanced diet." For example, an apple counts as "good" food, but a diet consisting of only apples is a very bad, unbalanced diet. Although items like cake are labeled "bad," something like a birthday cake should be enjoyed with family and friends and can be included occasionally as part of a balanced diet. No simple food in isolation is going to make a person fit or ruin his or her health. What matters more is how individual foods fit into an overall pattern of eating. The important thing is for each person to find a pattern that works for him or her, and to follow that pattern consistently.

We depend on food to survive. Only oxygen and water are more critical. Since preparing and eating food are essential components of our lives, we should consider bringing mindful awareness to this process. Shopping for food and preparing food can be occasions for mindfulness. During this process, take in the colors, textures, and aromas of different foods. Notice their taste and texture at different points in the cooking process. Feel the utensils in your hands, hear the sizzle in a pan on the stove, and notice how ingredients are transformed and melded together in the final dish. Cooking is truly a holistic art, and here's a secret: cooking is not solely for women or male chefs. All men should try their hand at it, and not only at a grill, but in the entire process. If one's spouse is willing, couples can enjoy one another's company in the kitchen, and cooking can be a full family affair. Some people believe that a cook's energy and spirituality are transferred into the food. Why not enhance that energy with togetherness and mutual enjoyment? Single people can also benefit by cooking mindfully, cultivating the art of preparing and eating food by enjoying the process, but also by remaining open to new influences and approaches.

Holistic Happiness

If you are like most people, when you are eating your mind is somewhere else, perhaps focused on the television, the computer, or something you are reading. Perhaps you are recalling conversations, memories, and thoughts of the day, or planning for the future. When this happens, you hardly notice the food you are placing in your mouth. As a result, you fail to enjoy the food and may tend to overeat. In addition to overeating, eating mindlessly or hurriedly can also cause physical problems. Eating mindfully allows you to savor and enjoy each bite, and is much better for your health and digestion. Many people who suffer from a sensitive stomach have learned that simply chewing their food longer and more slowly alleviates the intensity or frequency of discomfort.

In addition to eating mindlessly, snacking has become a concern. Humans have never snacked as they do today. According to Datamonitor, a company that analyzes food sales around the world, snacking now accounts for half of all "eating occasions" in the United States. People today not only snack more than their ancestors, but they also consume items for these snacks that their ancestors could never have imagined, such as chocolate-covered pretzels, Japanese nibbles flavored with wasabi, and energy balls made from dates and nuts that claim to be healthy even though they are sweeter than a brownie. If we no longer tell our children not to eat between meals, it may be partly because "between meals" takes up so much of our eating lives.

The increasing frequency of snacking since the 1970s means that many people are scarcely acquainted with the feeling of hunger anymore. Instead of sociable structured meals of breakfast, lunch, and dinner, the new pattern is a series of solitary snacks that we often fail to notice or enjoy. Without snacks and sugary drinks, which are effectively snacks in drinkable form, we would be eating far fewer calories than people did in the 1970s. Surprisingly, around a third of all calories consumed by the average American adult are now made up of snacks. Even those who think they don't snack much might mark their morning with a caffe latte and a biscotti and their afternoons with a protein bar. The food industry encourages us to feed every passing hunger with a bizarre range of snack products that earlier generations could never have imagined, let alone eaten.

It is worth noting, however, that some food cultures do not share disdain for snacks. A snack can be a noun or a verb. On the one hand, a snack can refer to a particular type of commercial snack food—ultra-processed and high in sugar, fat, and salt. But a snack can also refer to a way of eating:

a pattern of five or six modest-sized meals (as opposed to the pattern of two or three big ones many have grown up with). In some parts of the world, small eating events are considered so important that they are dignified with their own names and scheduled like other meals. This is true particularly in French- and Spanish-speaking worlds. Another country that views snacking positively is India, where no mother teaches her children not to eat between meals. Of course, this makes sense in a country where the greatest nutritional problem is not overnourishment but undernourishment. A few tasty snacks, which tend to be made from legumes or grains, can help add much-needed nutrients, especially for the country's many vegetarians. If all snacks were like these tasty Indian morsels, it's hard to see much wrong with snacking. Like tapas in Spain or bok choy in China, traditional Indian snacks can form a pleasurable and sociable pattern of eating that potentially contains a greater variety of flavors, textures, and even nutrition than the traditional Anglo-Saxon model of three square meals a day.

Many Americans gain weight in adulthood, increasing their risk for high blood pressure, heart disease, stroke, diabetes, certain types of cancer, arthritis, breathing problems, and other illnesses. Therefore, most adults should not gain weight. If you are overweight and have one of these problems, you should try to lose weight, or at the very least, not gain weight.

In all cases, learn to listen to your body to notice whether you are truly hungry or not, and if you are, be mindful of what foods you choose to eat. Be present to the chewing, tasting, and swallowing, and to when it's time to stop eating. Also bring awareness when you are inclined to eat for reasons other than hunger. If you are eating for emotional reasons, consider bringing self-inquiry to the emotions, rather than soothing them or dulling yourself with food. If you are eating or drinking for a quick energy boost or to change your mental state or mood, focus on your situation and understand the feelings that may fuel unhealthy habits. If you need energy, perhaps more rest or a regimen of healthy exercise is the answer.

Holistic Exercise

In order to stay at the same body weight, people must balance the number of calories in the foods and drinks they consume with the number of calories their body uses. Physical activity is an important way to use food energy. Most Americans spend much of their working day in activities that require little energy. In addition, many Americans of all ages now spend a lot of leisure time each day being inactive, involved in activities such as watching television or working at a computer. To burn calories, we need to devote less time to sedentary activities like sitting and spend more time in activities like walking to the store or around the block. When possible, we should use stairs rather than elevators. Less sedentary activity and more vigorous activity may help reduce body fat and lessen disease risk.

Reliable scientific evidence shows that adults begin to lose muscles mass at a rate of about 1 percent per year starting around age forty-five. The gradual loss is due to intrinsic aging and is called sarcopenia; loss of muscle mass is also caused by lack of exercise and protein deficiency. Fortunately, there are precautionary measures we can take to prevent or significantly delay the natural erosion of muscle mass. Participating in regular exercise is crucial. Someone once put it this way, "Regular physical activity is the closest thing to a miracle drug." Studies show that regular exercise by middle-aged individuals can set the clock back twenty to forty years when compared to those who are inactive. And evidence shows that it is never too late to start. Even people in their seventies and eighties can benefit significantly from moderate exercise.

When exercising or not, it is important at all times to sit and stand erect, with your back straight, abdomen drawn inward, shoulders back, and chest extended upward. In addition, imagine your head suspended by a cord from above. Good posture is critical to good health. As much as possible, avoid slouching, and whether you are afflicted by arthritis, kyphosis, or some other physical affliction, their effects can be reversed and even nullified through proper diet, exercise, therapy, and chiropractic care.

The human body is designed for movement, so we need to remain physically active if we want to keep our lives in balance. When the body is under stress or when our energy level seems depleted, exercise can improve its resilience and restore it to its normal equilibrium by releasing natural chemicals that build up during illness or under stress. Exercise yields the following benefits and performs the following functions:

- releases endorphins into our bloodstream creating a sense of well-being (some people call this the body's "natural high")
- decreases muscle tension caused by emotional stress and produces a relaxation response in our mind as well as in our body
- increases alpha-wave activity in the brain, thus allowing us to clear our mind so we can focus and concentrate more easily

- rids our body of toxins
- improves our overall flexibility and posture, thus decreasing spinal stiffness or pain caused by stress
- lessens fatigue and improves overall energy level
- produces more restful sleep
- provides a natural outlet for daily pressures and stress
- strengthens our heart and lungs, thus improving our overall physical fitness level and health
- increases our resting metabolism and can help us lose weight
- improves blood flow to the brain to nourish it with needed oxygen and help eliminate waste products
- reduces risk for those with stress-related medical conditions.

These results should be enough to motivate us to choose exercise as a primary means to improve our health and well-being.

As we consider exercising more or at least more wisely, there are three categories of exercise to consider, and if we want to achieve a fully balanced exercise program, all three categories play a role:

- *aerobic/cardiovascular*; these exercises are repetitive and rhythmic. They involve sustained use of the large muscles in the body, especially in our arms and legs. The goals of aerobic exercise are to strengthen our cardiovascular system and to increase our overall stamina. Popular aerobic exercises include running, jogging, brisk walking, swimming, bicycling, and dancing. If we walk less than two miles per day, we should consider ourselves inactive and begin our exercise program slowly. To round out our exercise program, we must make sure to include both stretching and toning exercises.
- *stretching/flexibility*; these exercises are neither vigorous nor prolonged enough to produce the cardiovascular strengthening that results from aerobic exercise. Instead, they are used to increase muscle strength and flexibility and to maintain healthy joints. If we live sedentary lives or if we are in poor physical condition, stretching and toning exercises will help prepare us for aerobic exercise with minimal risk of cardiovascular strain. Stretching exercises are slow, sustained, and relaxing. To be effective, stretches need to be held for at least thirty

seconds. Slow, sustained movements help us relax, but they also decrease muscle tension, improve circulation, and help prevent injury when used before and after aerobic exercise. Yoga is an example of a well-balanced exercise program.

- *toning/strengthening*; toning exercises utilize higher repetitions and lower weights to target muscles that need firming. Some good examples are crunches for stomach muscles, squats for thigh muscles, heel raises for calf muscles, and push-ups for arm and chest muscles. Muscle strengthening is a step beyond muscle toning. Here muscles are strengthened by using greater weights and fewer repetitions. There are three ways to strengthen muscles: concentrically (concentrics involve the *shortening* of muscles against resistance created by using free weights, resistance bands, or the use of resistive weight machines); isometrically (isometrics involve the *contraction* of muscles against resistance; they do not make muscles larger, but they do increase muscle strength); and eccentrically (eccentrics involve the lengthening of muscles against resistance). For example, walking down stairs requires eccentric lengthening of the quadricep muscles, whereas these same muscles are concentrically shortened in order to walk up stairs.

If exercise is important to you, then you will create space for it in your life. Remember that for a busy person, exercise is an important outlet for daily stress. Exercise gives you energy and helps keep your body fit, strong, and capable of handling what comes your way. If you need help or incentive to get started, you can join an exercise group or get together with a friend who already exercises regularly and who would encourage you to do so as well. Keep in mind that it is never too late to begin exercising, for exercise is for all ages and shapes.

Longevity and the New Prime of Life

In the late 1700s the average life expectancy at birth was 35 years. At the end of the nineteenth century, it was 47 years on average, and only 3 percent of the population made it past age 65. The twentieth-century revolution in longevity led to an added 25 or more years of life. In the United States, despite a drop from 79 in 2019 to 76.6 in 2021 due to COVID, average life expectancy at birth has jumped to 76 for males and 81 for females. In addition, people over 85 now constitute the fastest-growing segment of our population. Unfortunately, health maintenance and health promotion among the elderly population have not kept pace. Although it is true that we have postponed death, we have not yet been able to delay the age of onset of a variety of distressing disorders associated with growing older. Dementia, arthritis, diminished hearing and visual acuity, incontinence, and hip fracture all continue to occur at the same ages as in the past.

Does this mean that longer life necessarily brings with it more years of chronic disability? The latest evidence seems to support the concept that it does not and that we can defer disease and dysfunction. There are basically two ways of increasing longevity. One is through health promotion and disease prevention. The other is through basic research—involving all the rich new possibilities of molecular and cellular biology—and application of the results. However, we need not wait for the future findings of biology to apply what we already know.

Exercise, particularly aerobic activity and resistance training, has been shown to reduce physical frailty, yet 71 percent of people do not exercise. Additionally, disease prevention has increased significantly in the past fifty years; nevertheless many people do not get vaccines necessary to prevent such diseases as pneumonia and the many strains of the flu. Lung cancer attributable to tobacco use has surpassed breast cancer among women, yet nearly 23 percent of women still smoke. In fact, tobacco and alcohol are directly responsible for the top two causes of premature death—heart disease and cancer. Even so, there are 18 million Americans with alcohol problems, 10 million of whom are considered to have alcoholic disorders. In addition, the vast majority of Americans continue to eat high-fat diets, even though such foods have shown to dramatically increase the risks of heart disease and cancer. It is never too late to introduce new health habits. Indeed, the economic consequences of not doing so and, consequently, of not preventing or postponing dysfunction, are staggering.

Significantly, fifty is considered the new prime of life. At the turn of the twentieth century, one's thirties were looked upon as the key decade during the adult years, that is, the stage when a person was expected to mark his or her major achievements and enjoy the best of health and wisdom. By the middle of the twentieth century, the forties became one's prime decade. Today, thanks to the achievements of modern medicine and an unparalleled standard of living, we can expect our second fifty years to be as rich and full as the first. Of course, this does not mean that age does not bring changes, or that we can breeze through our mature years painlessly.

Nor does it change the fact that we live in a youth-oriented society. But today people in their sixties and even older run marathons, earn college degrees, start new businesses, travel around the world, and experience the enthusiasm and excitement of new ventures.

Successful Aging

Successful aging includes three main components: low probability of disease and disease-related disability, high cognitive and physical function capacity, and active engagement with life. Nevertheless, successful aging is more than absence of disease, important thought that is, and more than the maintenance of functional capacities. Both are important, but it is their combination of active engagement with life that represents the concept of successful aging most fully.

The previously held view that increased risk of diseases and disability with advancing age results from inevitable, intrinsic aging processes, for the most part genetically determined, is inconsistent with a developing body of information that many aging characteristics are due to lifestyle and are not age-dependent. Included among these are maintenance of interpersonal relations and of productive activities such as developing hobbies and unpaid volunteer work.

As we grow older, we face a remarkable number of changes in body composition, including reduction in lean body mass, which occurs primarily as a result of loss in skeletal muscle mass. Loss in muscle mass accounts for much of the energy loss characteristic of older people. In sedentary individuals, the main determinant of energy expenditure is fat-free mass, which declines by about 15 percent between the third and eight decades of life. If declining caloric needs are not matched by an appropriate decline in caloric intake, the ultimate result is increased body fat. This, together with increased abdominal obesity, is thought to be directly linked to the greatly increased incidence of type II diabetes in the elderly population.

Reduced muscle strength in older people is a major cause of the increased prevalence of the functional disability found in this population. Muscle strength forms a critical component of mobility, and the high prevalence of falls among institutionalized elders may be a consequence of reduced muscle strength. Over the past several decades, evidence has been accumulating to indicate that a positive correlation exists between physical activity and the reduction in risk of such chronic diseases as coronary heart disease, hypertension, and osteoporosis. As noted above, aerobic exercise is an important means of preventing and treating many of the chronic diseases typically associated with old age. If physical activity reduces the risk of developing these chronic diseases, it is logical to assume that premature mortality—from any cause—can be averted or at least delayed by physical activity. Consequently, physical activity can be expected to enhance longevity. While exercise cannot guarantee longevity to all, middle-aged individuals might expect to gain, on average, some two years of life from being physically active. It is encouraging to note that even older individuals do benefit from a physically active life and that the process of healthy aging can begin at any age.

Though endurance exercise has been the traditional means of increasing cardiovascular fitness, the American College of Sports Medicine currently recommends strength or resistance training as an important component of an overall fitness program. This is particularly important in the elderly population, where weakness and loss of muscle mass are prominent deficits. Strength conditioning or progressive resistance training involves few contractions against a heavy load. Muscle strength has been shown to increase in response to training between 60 and 100 percent of the maximum amount of weight that can be lifted with one contraction. The increased caloric need resulting from strength training may be a way for older people to improve their overall nutritional intake when the calories are chosen as nutrient-dense foods. In particular, calcium is an important nutrient to increase, since calcium intake is found to be one of the few nutrients limited in the diet of elderly men and women.

Virtually anyone can benefit from muscle strength training. As discussed above, the benefits of resistance training for older women and men are increased strength, increased muscle mass, improved balance, walking speed and ability to climb stairs, increased bone density, increased overall levels of physical activity, decreased protein requirements, improved glucose tolerance and decreased risk of type II diabetes, and increased energy. Furthermore, resistance exercise is a safe and important adjunct to a weight-loss program.

For older participants in resistance training, repetitions should be performed slowly through a full range of motion, allowing two or three seconds to lift the weight and four to six seconds to lower the weight. Performing the exercise more quickly will not enhance strength gains and may increase the risk of injury. The amount of weight that is lifted should increase as strength builds. This should take place every two to three weeks. Because advancing age results in increased muscle stiffness and reduced elasticity of connective tissue, proper warm-up and stretching can reduce the risk of orthopedic injury. A five-minute warm-up followed by five to ten minutes of slow stretching is highly recommended.

In view of the many sedentary adults living in the United States today, it seems sensible as an initial step to adopt the recommendation from the Centers for Disease Control and Prevention and the American College of Sports Medicine that "every U. S. adult should accumulate thirty minutes or more of moderate-intensity physical activity on most, preferably all, days of the week." A more realistic goal, I have discovered, is thirty minutes a day for five days a week. Rest and days off are important and beneficial. If your goal is to improve your health, studies in recent years consistently indicate that you get the most benefit when you go from no exercise to exercising moderately. In fact, most of the health benefits probably occur from mild exercise, not necessarily from the most arduous workouts.

The good news is that what researchers call moderate exercise really is moderate. Most health benefits seem to accrue if you simply walk briskly for about twenty to thirty minutes a day, covering a mile in fifteen to twenty minutes, or ride a bike at a modest pace or swim at a comfortable pace. Almost any physical activity will suffice, and there is no need to push yourself until you are gasping for air. You don't even need to return from your session soaked in sweat. Yes, you do get extra benefit from exercising harder or longer, but that benefit is small compared to the benefit you apparently get from moderate exercise. You can still get real cardiovascular benefit from an easy thirty-minute bike ride; however, the key with mild levels of activity is that they need to occur frequently. Instead of a long walk, you can take three ten-minute walks a day, or ride a bike for twenty minutes and walk for ten.

When it comes to benefits of strength training, the evidence shows that it can improve muscle strength, make everyday life easier, and prevent falls. Studies show that muscle that is developed with exercise is more efficient, has more mitochondria, and is better at using fat for fuel and at allowing cells to use insulin to utilize blood sugar, thus making diabetes less likely.

Another reason to exercise is to improve your appearance and your performance. You may want to be thinner, or stronger. In this case, moderate exercise is unlikely to be enough. Whether you want to lose weight may depend on how hard you exercise, how long, what you eat, and on your genetics. Obesity experts recommend brisk walking, but a half-hour or so at that pace burns around 150 calories. In a month, if you do not change your diet, you could lose up to a pound. It really is more effective to exercise hard enough to sweat, for that is the only way to burn large numbers of calories.

Whether you grow stronger or reshape your body depends on many factors, including genes but also how often you lift weights, whether the weights are heavy enough to stress your muscles, and whether you stay with your program. One thing is certain; the exercising that will make you thinner and more muscular requires not just consistency but effort. The biggest way to gain fitness is to push intensity.

In conclusion, while regular exercise is important for people of all ages, there is no group in our society that can benefit more from regularly performed exercise than older people. Though both aerobic and strength condition are highly recommended, only strength training can reduce age-related loss of muscle mass. Increased muscle strength and mass in an older person can be the first step toward a lifetime of increased physical activity and a realistic strategy for maintaining functional status and independence.

Once you start exercising, and get past the initial discomfort and frustration, you may discover you will not want to quit. Time and again, when people are asked why they keep exercising, they say that they kept at it because they discovered that they loved the routine. I can attest to that. Having cycled avidly most of my life; having begun a flexibility and stretching routine in my early thirties that I continue to this day; having participated in yoga and tai chi classes for years; and having jogged, cross-country skied, kayaked, hiked, or walked most of my life; I can say that exercise makes me feel exhilarated while keeping me healthy and focused. Over time, I have come to consider exercise as spiritual activity.

Questions for Discussion and Reflection

In addition to the questions listed at the end of the preface, answer the following questions, writing your answers in a journal. If you are in a group study, be prepared to share your answers with those in the group.

1. After reading this chapter, what did you learn about the correlation between holistic eating and the sacrament of the present moment?
2. In your estimation, what does Aristotle's teaching about the "mean" teach about holistic eating?

Holistic Happiness

3. After reading this chapter, what changes do you wish to make regarding your diet or your eating habits?
4. After reading this chapter, what did you learn about shopping mindfully? About cooking mindfully? About eating mindfully?
5. After reading this chapter, what did you learn about snacking?
6. If you exercise, which forms of exercise do you enjoy the most? Why?
7. If you exercise, which forms of exercise do you find most beneficial? Why?
8. After reading this chapter, what changes do you wish to make regarding exercising?
9. If you wish to add one aerobic/cardiovascular exercise to your workouts, what would it be?
10. If you wish to add one stretching/flexibility exercise to your workouts, what would it be?
11. If you wish to add one toning/strengthening exercise to your workouts, what would it be?

10

Holistic Creativity

CREATIVITY IS AN EXPERIENCE—A spiritual experience. At first, each of us receives a task: to be our unique selves by creating a life never before lived. As the painter Pablo Picasso quipped, "Every child is an artist. The problem is how to remain an artist when he (or she) grows up."

As a Christian, I affirm the biblical teaching that each human is made in the image of God. While some observers have defined this image as reason and others as conscience, the Self (the archetype of wholeness), or the capacity for compassion, love, or intimacy with the divine, some identify it as creativity or imagination.

According to seminal teacher and artist Julia Cameron, creative artists dwell in the presence of something transcendent—in the realm of spiritual electricity—and the heart of creativity is an experience of mystical union with a transcendent entity some call God but also Great Creator, Higher Power, Divine Spirit, Source, Mind, Universe, Deity, and Goddess. Like electricity, we don't need to understand Deity to utilize its power and grace. Those who speak in spiritual terms routinely refer to God as Creator and to themselves as co-creators or sub-creators, forging a creative alliance, artist-to-artist with the Great Creator. According to Cameron, accepting the following basic principles of creativity can greatly expand our creative possibilities:[1]

1. Creativity is the natural order of life, for life is pure creative energy.
2. There is an underlying, in-dwelling creative force infusing all life—including ourselves.

---

1. The following principles are adapted from Cameron, *Artist's Way*, 3.

3. When we open to our creativity, we open to the Creator's creativity within us.
4. As creations of God, we are meant to continue creativity by being creative.
5. Creativity is God's gift to us; using our creativity is our gift back to God.
6. Refusing to be creative is selfish and counter to our true nature.
7. When we explore our creativity, we open to God's orderly direction.
8. As we open our creative channel to the Creator, we can expect gentle yet powerful changes to our nature.
9. We are safe when we yield to ever-greater creativity.
10. Our creative dreams and yearnings come from a divine source; as we open to our dreams, we open toward our divinity.

Initiating our Creative Recovery

In her international bestseller *The Artist's Way*, a sourcebook on the subject of creativity, Cameron indicates that while all humans are creative by birth, many lose this innate ability, either through fear, compromise, or disuse. For those wishing to recover or to enable this gift, she recommends two task, which she labels "the morning pages" and "the artist date." A lasting creative awakening requires the consistent use of both.[2] By "morning pages," she refers to the process of writing three pages of longhand writing every day, strictly stream-of-consciousness. This exercise is not meant to be art or even proper writing, for there is no right or wrong way to do morning pages other than to write down whatever comes to mind. Nothing is too silly, stupid, or weird to be included. This material is meant to stimulate the brain, nothing more; and it is not intended for anyone except you. Cameron recommends that after writing each day, you should stick those pages in an envelope or in a spiral notebook and not read them for the first two months or so. To awaken your creativity, morning pages are non-negotiable. Just keep writing; if you can't think of anything to write, write "I can't think of anything to write." And when your internal Censor (who

---

2. I am indebted to Cameron for the material in this segment. While her book is intended as a guide for people pursuing artistic careers, the following ideas can be helpful for all individuals wishing to expand their creative abilities.

resides in your left brain) starts to criticize you or your writing, remember that these negative opinions are not the truth. It takes practice to learn to evade your Censor, so you must remember that there is no wrong way to write these pages. Write down your Censor's thoughts if you wish. If you or someone else asks, "Why do you write morning pages?" simply reply, "To get to the other side," by which you mean, to get to the other side of my fear, my negativity, or my moods.

In this regard, it is important to distinguish logic brain from artist brain. Logic brain thinks in neat, linear patterns. As a rule, it perceives the world according to known categories. Logic brain is our survival brain; it works on known principles. Anything new or unknown is perceived as wrong and possibly dangerous. Logic brain is our Censor; it is the voice we usually listen to, especially when we are telling ourselves to be sensible. Artistic brain is our inventor, our child. It says, "Wow! That is so neat!" Artistic brain is our creative, holistic brain. It follows hunches, is freewheeling, and regularly thinks "outside of the box." Morning pages are important for creativity because they teach logic brain to stand aside and let artist brain play.

It may be useful for you to think of morning pages as meditation. This may not be the practice of meditation to which you are accustomed. It may not seem spiritual or even meditative, but it is a valid form of meditation that gives us insight and helps us effect change in our lives. It is impossible to write morning pages for any extended period of time without coming into contact with an unexpected inner power. These pages become a trail that we follow into our own interior, where we meet both our own creativity and our Creator.

When Cameron first practiced writing morning pages, she was facing numerous disasters in her personal and professional life as a screenwriter. She wrote her pages faithfully, wondering what they meant, if anything. And then one morning, a character named Johnny strolled into her pages, and without planning, she found herself writing a novel. The morning pages had shown her the way. Now, whenever she feels stuck with a painful situation or problem she doesn't think she can handle, she goes to the pages and asks for guidance, for experience taught her that morning pages always connect us with a source of wisdom within.

According to Cameron, the other basic tool for connecting with one's inner creativity is "the artist date." Think of these tools in terms of a radio receiver and transmitter. When doing the morning pages, you are sending—that is, notifying yourself of your dreams, hopes, and frustrations.

When doing the artist date, you are receiving—that is, opening yourself to insight, inspiration, and guidance. An artist date is a block of time, perhaps two hours weekly, especially set aside and committed to nurturing your creative consciousness. Essentially, it is a play date that you preplan and defend against all interference. You do not take anyone on this artist date, only you and your inner artist (your creative child).

Recovering our Inner Creative Child

Your artist is a child. For children, time with a parent matters more than money spent. A visit to a junk store, a trip to the beach, watching an old movie, visiting a zoo or an art gallery, these can be opportunities for you to spend time alone with your inner child that is sacred. What children want is attention, not expensive outings. Spending time alone with your artist child is essential to self-nurturing. A long country walk, an expedition to the beach for a sunrise or sunset, a visit to a strange church to hear gospel music or to an ethnic neighborhood to encounter foreign sights and sounds—your artist may enjoy any of these.

Commit yourself to a weekly artist's date, and then watch your killjoy side try to wriggle out of it. Watch how this sacred time gets easily encroached upon. Watch how the sacred time suddenly includes a third party. Learn to guard against these invasions. By this I am not implying that you become antisocial or a loner, but only that if you wish to unleash your inner creativity, you set aside quality time for the artist child within. Having fun is your inner child telling you your art needs more playful inflow. A little fun can go a long way toward making your work feel more like play. Imaginative fun is at the heart of all creative work.

Art is an image-using system. In order to create, we draw from our inner well. This inner well, an artistic reservoir, is ideally like a well-stocked pond. It contains big fish, little fish, fat fish, skinny fish, fast-moving minnows and slow-moving ones—an abundance of artistic fish to fry. As artists, we need to maintain this artistic ecosystem. If we don't give it attention, our well is apt to become depleted, stagnant, or blocked. As artists, we must learn to be self-nourishing. This means we must become alert to consciously replenish our creative resources as we draw on them. Filling our well involves the active pursuit of images to stimulate and refresh our artistic reservoirs. Art is born in attention; its midwife is detail. Like birth, art can also spring from pain.

Holistic Creativity

In all the activity of our lives, we need to pay attention to the images that haunt us. Even in the midst of pain, these images can bring delight. Artists who tell you different are lying. The language of art is image, symbol. The artist's language is sensual, a language of felt experience. When we work at our art, we dip into the well of our experience and scoop out images. The artist brain cannot be reached—or triggered—effectively by words alone. The artist brain is the sensory brain; sight, sound, smell, taste, and touch, these are the elemental stuff of art. In the artistic process, it is important to remember to keep our well full. This requires filling it with images. To do so, think fun, think delight, think magic. Do not think duty, however. Duty can numb us, turn us off, tune out creativity. Rather, do what intrigues you, explore what interests you; think mystery, not mastery. Art is the imagination at play in the field of time. Let yourself play.

One of our primary needs as creative beings is support. Ideally, this can be nurtured and encouraged first by our nuclear family and then by ever-widening circles of friends, mentors, and well-wishers. Unfortunately, as creative individuals, many of us never receive this critical early encouragement. As a result, we may remain "shadow artists," not knowing we are artists at all. Shadow artists often choose shadow careers—those close to the desired art, even parallel to it, but not the art itself. As a rule, shadow artists judge themselves harshly, faulting themselves for not having acted on their dreams. This condemnation only reinforces their status as shadow artists. Remember, it takes nurturing to make an artist. Shadow artists do not receive sufficient nurturing, so unfortunately, they blame themselves. They want to write; they want to paint; they want to act, make music, and dance; but they are afraid to take themselves seriously. In order to move from the realm of shadows into the light of creativity, shadow artists must learn to take themselves seriously. Gently and deliberately, they must nurture their artist child. Creativity is play, but for shadow artists, learning to allow themselves to play is hard work.

Learning to let ourselves create is like learning to walk. The artist child must begin by crawling. Baby steps will follow, and there will be falls. Typically, recovering shadow artists will use these early efforts to discourage continued exploration. Like writing morning pages, don't judge your early artistic efforts by comparing them against other artists. In recovering from artistic blocks, it is necessary to go gently and slowly. What we are after here is the healing of old wounds, not the creation of new ones. Mistakes are necessary; stumbles are normal. Progress, not perfection, is what we should be asking of ourselves.

Artistic recovery is like marathon training. We want to log ten slow miles for every one fast mile. Recovery is an awkward, tentative, even embarrassing process. There will be many times when we won't look good—to ourselves or anyone else. However, it is impossible to get better and look good at the same time. Give yourself permission to be a beginner, and embrace the darkness. To be creative requires risks, trial and error, and learning from mistakes. Don't be afraid to confront negative notions about yourself and about what it means to be an artist. Begin by clearing away the negatives you have acquired from families, teachers, and friends. Negative beliefs are exactly that: beliefs, not facts. Then continue with affirmations. As you proceed, identify your passion, for it will tell you the direction you must follow to pursue your creative abilities. You may not be an artistic genius, and that's okay. Only a limited number of people have that kind of talent. The important thing is to identify, unleash, and cultivate the talent within. You can and will improve, but you must allow yourself that opportunity. Find mentors, and surround yourself with positive friends who encourage you and believe in you.

Expand your morning pages by creating lists of affirmations. Objections will start to pop up, but these may well come from your Censor, who loathes anything that sounds like authentic self-worth. Write down the rotten things your subconscious blurts out. Then compare them with your affirmations and do some detective work. When did these accusations and affirmations arise? One effective way to locate the sources of accusations and affirmations is to time-travel. Break your life into five-year increments, and list by name your major influencers in each time block. Where do your core beliefs come from? Who contributed to the shaping of your self-image? Don't be afraid to identify the villains in your life, but also the supporters who truly believed in you.

Trusting our creativity may be new behavior for many of us. This awkward, erratic feeling is a normal part of getting unstuck, of pulling free from the muck that has blocked us. There is a clear ebb and flow to the process of recovering our creative selves. As we gain strength, so will some of the attacks of self-doubt. This is normal, and we can deal with these attacks when we see them as symptoms of recovery. Early in our creative recovery, self-doubt can lure us into self-sabotage. A common form for this sabotage is showing someone our morning pages. If we show these to friends who are still blocked, their critique can sabotage our progress and keep us blocked. In this regard, it is important that we not surround ourselves with people whose creativity is blocked. Our recovery can threaten them, and they may be quick to respond with criticism. Refuse to allow their doubt or negativity to turn into self-sabotage.

The essential element in nurturing our creativity lies in nurturing ourselves. Through self-nurture we nurture our inner connection to the Great Creator. Through this connection our creativity will unfold. Paths will appear for us. We need to trust the Great Creator and move out in faith. Soon enough, we will become bridges that will allow others to cross from self-doubt into self-expression. As our recovery progresses, we will learn that it is actually easier to write than not write, paint than not paint, and so forth. We will learn to enjoy the process of being a creative channel and to surrender our need to control the result. We will discover the joy or practicing our creativity. The process, not the product, will become our focus. Our own progress is the greatest message of hope for others.

Having discussed the barrier to recovery others and even our internal Censors can present, let us look at another inner enemy, skepticism. Perhaps the greatest barrier for any of us as we look for an expanded life is our own deeply held skepticism, which we might call our secret doubt. It does not seem to matter whether we are officially believers or agnostics. We have our doubts about this creator/creativity notion, and those doubts are very powerful. Many times in life we sweep our feelings of doubt "under the rug." We need to stop doing that and explore them instead.

Our secret doubt works something like this: "Okay, so I started writing morning pages and I seem more awake and alert in my life. So what? It's just a coincidence. But am I really talented? Do I have a creative bent? Not really." With this attitude firmly entrenched, we not only look all gift horses in the mouth, but also swat them on the rump to get them out of our lives as fast as possible. One of the things worth noting in a creative recovery is our reluctance to take seriously the possibility that the universe just might be cooperating with our new and expanded plans. If we think of our mind as a room in which we keep all our usual ideas about life, God, and what's possible and what's not, picture that room with a door slightly ajar. Outside the room is a great deal of dazzling light, with a lot of new ideas that we consider impractical or impossible. Should we shut the door tight, or open it a bit more? The latter possibility is what makes for open-mindedness. Begin, this week, consciously practicing opening the door of your mind to new opportunities and possibilities.

Holistic Happiness

If you feel stuck in your life or in your art, few jump starts are more effective than a week of deprivation from reading, television, media, news outlets, or other compulsive or routine entertainment or information. While such deprivation might seem impossible, it is actually necessary. Without distractions from reading and media, we are once again thrust into the fullness of our sensory world. This gives us a chance to spend more time outdoors, or in museums, art galleries, or walking through ethnic neighborhoods. Reading and media deprivation can also cast us into our inner silence, a space some of us might begin to fill with new possibilities. For a long time, many of us have been too busy to hear our own inner voice, the voice of our artist's inspiration, above the static. In practicing reading and media deprivation, we need to cast a watchful eye on additional pollutants in our life that poison our well. If we monitor the inflow and keep it to a minimum, we will be rewarded for our deprivation with embarrassing speed. Our reward will be a new outflow. Our own art, our own thoughts and feelings, will begin to nudge aside the sludge of blockage, to loosen it and move it outward until once again our well is running freely.

Creativity and Spirituality

One of the chief barriers to accepting God's generosity is our limited notion of what we are able to accomplish. We may tune in to the voice of the Creator within, hear a message, and then discount it as impossible. It is understandable that we might not want to look like idiots pursuing grandiose schemes. However, if we don't take ourselves—or God—seriously enough, we might define as impossible opportunities that, with God's help, may fall withing our grasp. Remembering that God is our source, we are in the spiritual position of having an unlimited bank account. Most of us never consider how powerful the Creator is, and thereby draw very limited amounts of the power available to us. When we decide how powerful God is for us, we unconsciously set limits on how much God can give us or help us. And if we receive gifts beyond our imagining, we often send them back.

I m not talking here of faith as magic or wish-fulfillment, but more about a conscious partnership in which we work slowly and gradually clearing away the wreckage of our negative partnering, clarifying the vision of what it is we want, and learning to accept small pieces of that vision until one day the vision falls into place. In other words, we must pray to catch the bus, and then run as fast as we can to get onboard. For this to

Holistic Creativity

happen, we must believe that we are allowed to catch the bus. When we do, we come to recognize that God is unlimited in supply and that everyone has equal access. This begins to clear up guilt about getting or asking too much. Since everyone can draw on this universal supply, we deprive no one with our abundance. If we learn to think of receiving God's good gifts as an act of worship—cooperating with God's plan to manifest goodness in our lives—we can begin to let go of having to sabotage ourselves.

Creativity is a spiritual issue. Any progress we make is by leaps of faith, some small and some large. And that faith begins with taking the first step toward learning a new medium. Later, that faith may lead to classes, seminars, and possibly a year's sabbatical. Still later we may conceive an idea for a book, or artistic space in an art gallery exhibit. If this sounds unreachable, ask yourself bluntly what steps you are evading and what dreams you are discounting. With God as our source, all things are possible. In the Sermon on the Mount, Jesus encourages his followers to seek first God's kingdom (God's will), and all other things will be given to them as well (Matt 6:33). Sometimes we limit "all other things" to the realm of spirituality, but to do so is to go against the context of the passage. God is not a stern parent with rigid ideas about what's socially acceptable or politically correct. God wants us to live life fully, and that certainly implies areas such as creative writing, art, and dance. Living artistically means getting into the now and enjoying our day. It begins with giving ourselves treats and breaks. God is a God of extravagance and abundance, and we should learn to be extravagant with ourselves and with others. As we expect God to be more generous, God will be more generous to us.

Artists must develop the ability to listen, an ability we hone in the practice of morning pages and artist dates. The pages train us to hear past our Censor. The artist dates help us to pick up the voice of inspiration. While both activities are apparently unconnected with the actual act of making art, they are critical to the creative process. Art is not about thinking something up, but about the opposite—getting something down. If we try to think something up, we are straining to reach for that which is beyond our grasp. If we get something down, there is no strain. Now we are not focused on doing, but on getting. Someone or something else is doing the doing. In the creative process, instead of reaching for inventions, we are engaged in listening.

When actors are in the moment, they are engaged in listening creatively for the next right thing. When painter's paint or sculptors sculpt, they are often letting the brush take the next stroke or the marble block to unveil its figure. In dance, composition, or art, the experience is the same; we are more the conduit than the creator of what we express. This can be said of all art. If painting and sculptures wait for us, then sonatas wait for us, and books, plays, and poems wait as well. Our job is simply to get them down. Art is like dropping down the well, living beneath the surface of our normal consciousness. Like an underground river, inspiration flows through us as a stream of ideas that we can tap down into. As artists, our job is to drop down the well into the stream. Some people find it easier to picture the stream of inspiration like radio waves being broadcast at all times. With practice, we learn to hear the desired frequency on request or tune to the frequency we want.

Once we accept that it is natural to create, we can begin to accept a second idea—that the Creator will hand us whatever we need for the project. The minute we are willing to accept the help of this collaborator, we begin to see useful bits of help everywhere in our lives. If we remember that God is the Great Artist, then we can expect the universe to support our dream.

One of the great obstacles to the creative process is perfectionism. Perfectionism has little to do with getting things right. It is actually a barrier, a refusal to let ourselves move forward. Perfectionism is a loop—an obsessive, debilitating closed system that causes us to get stuck in the details of what we are writing or painting or making and to lose sight of the whole. Instead of creating freely and allowing errors to reveal themselves as insights, we often become mired in getting the details right. We correct our originality into a uniformity that lacks passion and spontaneity. "Do not fear mistakes," jazz trumpeter Miles Davis noted. "There are none."

The perfectionist fixes one line of a poem over and over—until no lines are right. The perfectionist writes so many versions of scene one that she never gets to the rest of the play. Instead of enjoying the process, the perfectionist is constantly grading the results. "A painting is never finished. It simply stops in interesting places," said Paul Garner. A book is never finished, nut at a certain point we stop writing it and go on to the next book. A film is never cut perfectly, but at a certain point we let go and call it done. That is a normal part of creativity and of all spirituality—letting go.

This brings us to the topic of risk. Most of us make a practice of talking ourselves out of risk. However, risk, including trial and error, are part of all worthy endeavors. In order to risk, we must jettison our accepted limits, including limits such as age, personality, and ability. Usually, when we say we can't do something, what we mean is that we won't do something unless we can guarantee success. Working artists know the folly of this stance. There is a common joke among directors: "Oh, yeah. I always know exactly how I should direct the picture—after I'm done directing it."

As blocked artists, we unrealistically expect and demand success from ourselves and recognition of that success from others. With that as an unspoken demand, a great many things remain outside our sphere of possibility. As actors, we tend to allow ourselves to be typecast rather than working to expand our range. As singers, we stay married to safe material. As songwriters, we try to repeat a formula hit. In this way, artists who do not appear blocked to outside observers experience themselves as blocked internally, unable to take the risk of moving into new and more satisfying artistic territory.

Creativity is often scary, because in all careers there are setbacks and U-turns. Sometimes these setbacks become opportunities to recycle. Like coming up to a difficult equestrian jump, sometimes we need to circle a few times before trying the fence again. Successful ventures are often built on setbacks or on successful failures. In the summer of 1989, when I finished cycling across the continental United States, I had planned to continue my sabbatical semester with a trip across Europe and the Middle East, investigating ancient archaeological sites. Early that summer, prior to my cycling venture, I had contacted a travel specialist, and we had gone over the details of my planned trip abroad. However, when I finished cycling and contacted my travel agent again, I learned that her office had been flooded and nothing had been done regarding my trip. Able to procure a couple of visas beforehand, I had to plan the trip on the fly, for I was scheduled to depart three weeks later. Fortunately, arranging my own travel led to an in-depth experience that culminated in my book *Into Thin Places*. Had the trip been planned professionally, I would not have encountered the setbacks, detours, and U-turns that made possible the writing of that book and likely my ensuing writing career, for my experience would have lacked depth, vitality, and spontaneity.

Creativity is God energy flowing through us, shaped like light flowing through a crystal prism. When we are clear about who we are and what we are doing, the energy flows freely. However, when we resist what that energy might show us and where it might take us, we often experience out-of-control feelings. We want to shut down the flow and regain our sense of control. We slam on the psychic brakes.

We all deal with creative energy in unique ways. But what happens when that energy feels blocked? For some people, food is a creative issue. Eating sugar or fats or certain carbohydrates may seem like a solution, but that only leaves them feeling dull and shaky. They use food to block energy and change. As the shaky feeling comes that they are going too fast or are about to fly apart, these people reach for food. A big bowl of ice cream, an evening of junk food, and their system clogs. For some people alcohol is the favored block, or drugs. For many, work is the block of choice. Overly busy, they grab for additional tasks. They find they don't have time for family, friends, or even for themselves. Others, obsessed with painful love, reach for painful experiences, only to be left feeling like victims.

Please note that food, work, and sex are all good in themselves. It is the abuse of them that makes them blockers of creativity. Knowing ourselves as artists means acknowledging which of these we abuse when we want to block ourselves. Sensing our real potential and the wide range of possibilities open to us scares us. Thus, we all reach for blocks to slow our growth. If we are honest with ourselves, we all know which blocks are toxic. When asked to name our poison, most of us can. "Has food sabotaged my creativity, or workaholism, or sex, or love obsession?" Blocking is essentially a lack of faith. Rather than trust our intuition, talent, skill, or desire, we fear where our Creator is taking us with creativity. Rather than paint, write, dance, or audition to see where they take us, we insert a block. For most us, happy is unfamiliar, out of control, risky, and even terrifying.

In any creative life we have dry spells. These droughts appear from nowhere and stretch to our horizon. Life loses its sweetness, and our work feels mechanical, empty, and forced. We feel we have nothing to say, and are tempted to say nothing. These are the times when the morning pages are most difficult and yet most valuable. During a drought, we are fighting with God. We have lost faith—in the Great Creator and in our creative selves. Thankfully, droughts end. They end because we refuse to quit. We may have doubted, but we stumble on. In a creative life, droughts are necessary. The time in the desert brings us clarity and charity. When we are in a creative drought, we need to know there is a purpose. At such times, we must keep writing morning pages, for they are both our wilderness and our path forward.

Never forget: creativity is its own reward. As artists, we must surround ourselves with people who nurture our artistic self, not with people who try to overly domesticate us for our own good. Certain friendships will enhance our artistic imagination, but others can deaden it. To a large degree, our life is our art, and when it gets dull, so does our work. As artists, our self-respect comes from doing the work, not from what others think. There is a connection between self-nurturing and self-respect. If we allow ourselves to be troubled by those who wish to have us conform, we sell ourselves out. They may like us better if we conform, but we will not. If we sabotage our inner artist, we can well expect an eating binge, a sex binge, an anger binge, or a mood binge. When artists are not creating, they are not always normal or nice—to themselves or to others.

Creativity is oxygen for the soul. Cutting off creativity makes people unhappy, depressed, or angry. When well-meaning parents and friends push marriage or nine-to-five jobs on them, artists react as if they are fighting for their lives, for they are. To be an artist is to question accepted standards, to recognize the particular, to appreciate the peculiar. To be an artist is to acknowledge the astonishing. It is to allow the wrong piece in a room if we like it, or to cling to a weird coat, hat, or other piece of clothing that makes us happy. If we are happier writing than not writing, painting than not painting, singing than not singing, dancing than not dancing, acting than not acting, the by all means we must allow ourselves to do it. To kill our dreams because they are irresponsible is to be irresponsible to ourselves. Credibility lies with us and God—not with votes of approval from others.

The Creator made us creative. Our creativity is our gift from God. Our use of it is our gift to God. Accepting this bargain is the beginning of true self-acceptance. How do we create? We learn by going where we have to go and by doing what we have to do. Exercise is often the going that moves us from stagnation to inspiration, from problem to solution, from self-pity to self-respect. Seemingly without effort, our answers come while we swim or cycle or run. When we go and do, we learn we are stronger than we thought. We learn to look at things with a new perspective. We learn to solve problems by tapping into our inner resources and listening for inspiration.

As we have noted, creativity requires faith, and faith requires that we relinquish control. This is frightening, and we resist it. Our resistance to our creativity is a form of self-destruction. We throw up roadblocks on our own path. Why do we do this? In order to maintain an illusion of control. Each of us has an inner dream that we can realize if we just have the courage to admit what it is. Our resistance to our creativity is quite understandable. We are not accustomed to think that God's will for us and our own inner dreams can coincide. The truth is that we are meant to live bountifully. The universe will always support affirmative action. Our truest dream for ourselves is always God's will for us. There is a path for each of us. By going, doing, and being—by trusting—we *learn* to trust.

Creativity—like all human life—begins in darkness. All too often we think only in terms of light, but it is true that insight often comes in hunches. Some of our greatest ideas and insights are preceded by a gestation period that is interior, murky, and completely necessary. Ideas, like stalagmites and stalagmites, form in the dark inner cave of our consciousness. They form in drips and drops, not in squared-off building blocks. We must learn to wait for ideas to emerge. Or, to use a gardening image, we must learn not to pull our ideas up by the roots to see if they are growing. Hatching an idea is like baking bread. An idea needs to rise. If you poke at it too much at the beginning, it will never rise. A loaf of bread must stay for a long time in the darkness and safety of the oven. Open that oven too soon and the bread collapses. The truth is that this is how to raise the best ideas. We must let them grow in dark and mystery, trusting their slow and seemingly random drip.

The artist's way is a spiritual journey, a pilgrimage home to the self. Like all great journeys, it entails dangers of the trail. Like all pilgrims, we will often be graced by fellow travelers and invisible companions. When we experience creativity, the disruption might make us feel we are losing our mind—or gaining our soul. Life is meant to be an artist date. That's why we were created.

Creativity and Healthy Aging

Creativity is not simply for the young or for those engaged in family life or career. Developing new skills adds to one's ability to adapt with aging, thereby promoting the maintenance of independent functioning. Recognizing the capacity to learn new strategies and develop creative dimensions in the face of loss expands rehabilitation potential for older adults and focuses not only on treating problems and fostering new strengths but also on restoring function and well-being. At a societal level, the role of older persons as a resource has historically been apparent in the wide spectrum of their contributions, ranging from the sharing of wisdom to volunteerism to helping younger members of their extended families.

Holistic Creativity

Examples of creativity in later life abound. Picasso remained prolific as a painter until he died in his nineties; Verdi composed his opera *Falstaff* at age 80; Edison kept inventing until his death in his eighties; Benjamin Franklin achieved heroic stature internationally as a diplomat in his seventies; Eubie Blake, the outstanding pianist and composer of ragtime music and show tunes, continued in great demand as a performer well into his nineties; and Grandma Moses, who lived to 101, turned to painting at the age of 78. The list goes on, as does the variation in the ways creativity is expressed among older adults.

While creativity is not an easy concept to define, we recall the eight intelligences Howard Gardner identified. In speaking of personal intelligence—knowledge of self and others—he cited the views of the British psychologist N. K. Humphrey who made the bold claim that the chief creative use of human intellect lies not in the traditional areas of art and science but rather in holding society together. In this respect, the creative situation of "elders" is discussed not only in terms of transferring personal knowledge to younger individuals, but from a developmental perspective where, with aging, one might acquire more fully developed knowledge of self and of others. American psychologist Abraham Maslow divided creativity into two types: "special talent creativity" and "self-actualizing creativeness." When, therefore, we see men or women in their later years who maintains a questing spirit, and who do so with courage and resourcefulness in a wide variety of circumstances, such men or women may well be seen as "Ulyssean adults."

Ancient Greek mythology talks about Tiresias, the citizen of Thebes who suffered the misfortune of viewing the goddess Athena while she was undressing to bathe. In a burst of rage, Athena blinded Tiresias. However, Zeus took pity on the mortal and replaced Tiresias's loss of outer vision with great insight and prophetic powers that grew over the years and facilitated long life for the seer.

It is my hope that institutions of learning, together with psychologists, counselors, and the community at large will recognize and respond to the opportunities offered by older citizens by putting in place programs and attitudes that nurture their vast and changing creative forces. Through such a shift in perspective, we can hope more readily to associate "creativity" with "aging" in generations to come.

Questions for Discussion and Reflection

In addition to the questions listed at the end of the preface, answer the following questions, writing your answers in a journal. If you are in a group study, be prepared to share your answers with those in the group.

1. Describe your creative impulses as a child. With regards to your creativity at that time, were you encouraged, discouraged, or simply left to your own devices?
2. Assess Julia Cameron's notion that creative artists dwell in the presence of transcendence.
3. Assess Julia Cameron's notion that creativity is the natural order of life.
4. Assess Julia Cameron's notion that refusing to be creative is selfish and counter to our true nature.
5. Assess the merit of Cameron's recovery tasks, namely, "the morning pages" and "the artist date." Have you experimented with either of these approaches or used them as training for new tasks and opportunities? If so, explain their usefulness. If not, explain why you have ignored such resources.
6. Explain the role of our internal Censor in discouraging our creative attempts or impulses.
7. In your estimation, which creative experience do you hold in highest esteem? Explain your answer.
8. Explain the role of our "inner well" and how it both contributes to or blocks our creativity.
9. After reading this chapter, what did you learn about the correlation between spirituality and creativity?
10. After reading this chapter, what memories did it trigger about experiences with creativity? Were they good, bad, or neither? Explain your answer.
11. After reading this chapter, what did you learn about how to enhance your inner creativity?
12. After reading this chapter, where do you wish to begin to express or develop your creativity? In your answer, be realistic, but also as precise as possible.

Bibliography

Albers, Susan. *Eating Mindfully*. 2nd edition. Oakland, CA: New Harbinger, 2012.
Borg, Marcus, and N. T. Wright. *The Meaning of Jesus: Two Visions*. San Francisco: HarperSanFrancisco, 2000.
Cameron, Julia. *The Artist's Way: A Spiritual Path to Higher Creativity*. 10th anniversary ed. New York: Tarcher/Putnam, 2002.
Coulston, Ann M., and Carol J. Boushey. *Nutrition in the Prevention and Treatment of Disease*. 2nd edition. Burlington, MA: Elsevier, 2008.
Coan, Richard. *Hero, Artist, Sage or Saint?* New York: Columbia University Press, 1977.
Crocker, Sylvia Fleming. *A Well-Lived Life: Essays in Gestalt Therapy*. Cleveland: Gestalt Institute, 1999.
Dalai Lama, and Howard C. Cutler. *The Art of Happiness: A Handbook for Living*. New York: Riverhead, 1009.
———. *The Art of Happiness at Work*. New York: Riverhead, 2003.
Davis, Martha, et al. *The Relaxation & Stress Reduction Workbook*. 6th edition. Oakland, CA: New Harbinger, 2008.
Dychtwald, Ken. *Healthy Aging: Challenges and Solutions*. Gaithersburg, MD: Aspen, 1999.
Eckhart, Meister. *Meister Eckhart*. Translated by R. B. Blakney. New York: Harper & Brothers, 1941.
Edelson, Paul Jay, and Patricia L. Malone. *Enhancing Creativity in Adult and Continuing Education*. San Francisco: Jossey-Bass, 1999.
Fowler, James. *Stages of Faith: The Psychology of Human Development and the Quest for Meaning*. San Francisco: HarperSanFrancisco, 1995.
Fox, Matthew. *Original Blessing*. Santa Fe, NM: Bear, 1983.
Glei, Jocelyn K. *Manage Your Day-to-Day: Build Your Routine, Find Your Focus, and Sharpen Your Creative Mind*. Las Vegas, NV: Amazon, 2013.
Hanh, Thich Nhat. *Good Citizens*. Berkeley, CA: Parallax, 2012.
———. *Living Buddha, Living Christ*. Rev. ed. New York: Riverhead, 2007.
Harris, Dan R. *Diet and Nutrition Sourcebook*. Detroit: Omnigraphics, 1996.
Haught, John. *Deeper Than Darwin: The Prospect for Religion in the Age of Evolution*. Boulder, CO: Westview, 2003.

Bibliography

———. *God After Darwin: A Theology of Evolution*. Boulder, CO: Westview, 2000.
———. *The Promise of Nature: Ecology and Cosmic Purpose*. Mahwah, NJ: Paulist, 1993.
———. *Responses to 101 Questions on God and Evolution*. Mahwah, NJ: Paulist, 2001.
———. *What is God? How to Think About the Divine*. Mahwah, NJ: Paulist, 1986.
Jung, Carl G. *Jung's Letters*. Vol 1. Edited by Gerhard Adler and Aniela Jaffé. Princeton, NJ: Princeton University Press, 1975.
———. *Memories, Dreams, Reflections*. New York: Pantheon, 1963.
———. *Modern Man in Search of a Soul*. New York: Harcourt, Brace and World, 1933.
Kasser, Tim. *The High Price of Materialism*. Cambridge, MA: The MIT Press, 2002.
Katerndahl, David A. "Impact of Spiritual Symptoms and Their Interactions on Health Services and Life Satisfaction." *Annals of Family Medicine* 6 (2008), 412–20. Online: www.annfammed.org/content/6/5/412.
Kelsey, Morton T. *Afterlife: The Other Side of Dying*. New York: Crossroad, 2005.
———. *Caring: How Can We Love One Another?* New York: Paulist, 1981.
———. *Christianity as Psychology: The Healing Power of the Christian Message*. Minneapolis: Augsburg, 1986.
———. *Companions on the Inner Way: The Art of Spiritual Guidance*. New York: Crossroad, 1983.
———. *Encounter with God: A Theology of Christian Experience*. Minneapolis: Bethany, 1972.
———. *Healing and Christianity*. Minneapolis: Augsburg, 1995.
Lamott, Anne. *Plan B: Further Thoughts on Faith*. New York: Riverhead, 2005.
Lappé, Frances Moore. *Diet for a Small Planet*. 20th anniversary edition. New York: Ballantine, 1991.
Lawrence, Brother. *The Practice of the Presence of God*. Mount Vernon, NY: Peter Pauper, 1963.
Lewis, C. S. *The Problem of Pain*. New York: Macmillan, 1962.
Lovin, Robin W. *Christian Ethics: An Essential Guide*. Nashville, TN: Abingdon, 2000.
May, Gerald. *Care of Mind, Care of Spirit*. San Francisco: Harper & Row, 1982.
Peck, M. Scott. *The Road Less Traveled*. New York: Simon & Schuster, 1978.
Rohr, Richard. *Falling Upward: A Spirituality for the Two Halves of Life*. San Francisco: Jossey-Bass, 2011.
———. *Immortal Diamond: The Search for Our True Self*. San Francisco: Jossey-Bass, 2013.
———. *The Naked Now: Learning to See as the Mystics See*. New York: Crossroad, 2009.
Saad, Marcelo, et al. "Are We Ready for a True Biopsychosocial-Spiritual Model? The Many Meanings of Spiritual." No pages. Online: https://www.mdpi.com/2305-6320/4/479/htm.
Smith, Huston. *Forgotten Truth: The Common Vision of the World's Religions*. San Francisco: HarperSanFrancisco, 1976.
Stahl, Bob, and Elisha Goldstein. *A Mindfulness-Based Stress Reduction Workbook*. Oakland, CA: New Harbinger, 2010.
Steere, Douglas V. *Spiritual Counsel and Letters of Baron Friedrich von Hügel*. New York: Harper & Row, 1964.
Sulmasy, Daniel P. "A Biopsychosocial-Spiritual Model for the Care of Patients at the End of Life." *Gerontologist* 42:3 (2002), 24–33.
Thompson, Edward H., Jr., and Lenard W. Kaye. *A Man's Guide to Healthy Aging: Stay Smart, Strong, and Active*. Baltimore: The Johns Hopkins University Press, 2013.

Bibliography

Tolle, Eckhart. *The Power of Now: A Guide to Spiritual Enlightenment*. Novato, CA: New World Library, 1999.
Tournier, Paul. *Creative Suffering*. San Francisco: Harper & Row, 1983.
Underhill, Evelyn. *Mysticism: A Study in the Nature and Development of Man's Spiritual Consciousness*. Rev. ed. New York: Dutton, 1961.
Vande Kappelle, Robert P. *Beyond Belief*. Eugene, OR: Wipf & Stock, 2012.
———. *Dark Splendor*. Eugene, OR: Wipf & Stock, 2015.
———. *In the Potter's Workshop*. Eugene, OR: Wipf & Stock, 2019.
———. *Into Thin Places*. Eugene, OR: Resource, 2010.
Weiss, Robert J., and Genell J. Subak-Sharpe. *Complete Guide to Health and Well-Being After 50*. New York: Times, 1988.
White, Timothy P. *The Wellness Guide to Lifelong Fitness*. New York: Rebus, 1993.
Wilson, Bee. *The Way We Eat Now*. New York: Basic, 2019.

Index

Abraham (patriarch), 8, 23
aging, 148–50
    successful, 150–53
Aristotle, 78
    and "the mean," 78, 142
"artist child," 158, 159, 162
artist date, 156, 158, 168
Augustine (bishop), 61

Berry, Wendell, 25
Bible. *See* scripture
body, ix, 18, 33, 49, 50, 54, 55, 56, 136
Boom, Corrie ten, 29
Borg, Marcus, 65–66
Brother Lawrence, 25
Buber, Martin, 60, 132
Buddha, Buddhism, 33, 40, 72, 79, 83, 95, 133–38
Buechner, Frederick, 60

Cameron, Julia, 155–58
Castro, Fidel, 29
Catherine of Siena, 18
Caussade, Jean Pierre de, 141
Churchill, Winston, 35
Coan, Richard, 75
compassion, 83, 86, 94, 99, 101, 110, 112, 114, 134, 138
consumerism, 124–38

consumption
    holistic, 124–38
    sensory, 134
conversion, religious. *See* second birth
Costa, Jess Dale, 43–46
creativity, 35–36, 37, 75
    and aging, 168–69
    and faith, 167
    holistic, 155–69
    and perfectionism, 164
    and spirituality, 155–56, 161, 162–68
Cutler, Howard, 111

Dalai Lama, 81, 111
D'Arcy, Paula, 60
Davis, Miles, 164
Dillard, Annie, 25
dispensationalism, 40
dualism, dualist, 10, 11, 12, 13, 14, 46, 136

eating, 133–34, 166
    holistic, 142–45
    sacramental, 140–42
Eckhart, Meister, 18, 97
Einstein, Albert, 68
Engel, George L., ix
Erikson, Erik, 1, 3
ethics. *See* morality
evil, 24–25, 26, 36, 76

Index

exercise
  benefits of, 146–47
  holistic, 145–53
  and longevity, 148–50
  types of, 147–48

faith, 3–4, 8, 13, 15, 27, 28, 35, 50, 52, 61, 105, 167
first half of life (phase 1A, 1B), 5, 9, 10–12, 92
five halves of life, 9–16
food. *See* eating
Fowler, James, 3, 4, 10, 11, 12, 15
Francis of Assisi, 18, 35, 138
Freud, Sigmund, 58, 85
Fromm, Erich, 93, 125

Gadamer, Hans-Georg, 59
Gardner, Howard, 169
Garner, Paul, 164
God, 14, 15, 19, 20, 23, 27, 31, 34, 35, 36, 37, 44, 45, 48, 51–52, 56, 79, 83
  existence of, 60–61
  image of, 155
  images of, 62, 68–69
  knowing and loving, 95
  as Life, 73
  neuter images of, 59–60
  as personal, 57–58, 60, 73n2
  as source of creativity, 155–56, 162–68
  terms for, 155
  as transpersonal, 58, 60
  as Trinity, 61
Golden Rule, 105
Great Commandment, 7, 97

Hanh, Thich Nhat, 79
happiness, 136–37
  definition of, 80
  and desire, 81–82
  as "everlasting life," 78
  holistic, 72–87
  and intimacy, 92–94
  and pleasure, 82, 117
  as purpose or success, 77, 80–81, 117
  and wealth, 113–14
Haught, John F., 58–59

healing
  holistic, 39–52
health, healthy, ix, 1, 39
  definition of, x
  and spirituality, 39–40
Heidegger, Martin, 59
Hindu(ism), 6–7, 10, 11, 12, 15, 40, 95
Hobbs, Thomas, 85
Holy Spirit, 12, 16, 19, 33, 41, 51, 56, 61, 66–68, 79, 102
Hügel, Friedrich von, 29–30
Humphrey, N. K., 169

imagination, 26, 37, 155, 159, 167
"inner well," 158
intimacy, 92–94
  definition of, 93
Islam, 40, 96

Jesus Christ, 7, 24, 25, 26, 28, 30, 32, 33, 51, 61, 62–63, 66, 74, 79, 96, 97, 98, 99, 104–5, 163
  as androgynous, 66
  as archetype, 66
  and discipleship, 96
  divinity of, 65, 66
  and gender, 102–3
  healing ministry of, 40–43
  humanity of, 63–65
  as lens, 65–66
  as Paraclete, 67
  and sacramental theology, 140–42
  as "wisdom of God," 79
Job, book of, 23, 24, 30
Judaism, 22, 63, 64, 96
Jung, Carl, 34, 66, 75–76, 97
  and personality theory, 89–92

Kasser, Tim, 126, 127
Katerndahl, David A., x
Kelsey, Morton, 101
Kierkegaard, Søren, 7–8, 9, 78
Kohlberg, Lawrence, 1, 3, 10, 11, 12, 15
Kübler-Ross, Elisabeth, 27–28

Lamott, Annie, 29
Lewis, C. S., 48

176

Index

listening, art of, 100–102
love, 14, 15, 16, 25, 41, 56, 61, 75, 82, 83, 95–100
    definition of, 95
Lovin, Robin, 74–75
loving
    enemies, 104–5
    holistic, 89–106
    strangers, 105

Maslow, Abraham, 125, 169
materialism, 125–33
    and drug abuse, 127, 130
    and unhappiness, 128, 129, 130
May, Gerald, 19
Merton, Thomas, 32
mind, ix, 18–19, 33, 50, 55, 56
    and happiness, 80–87
mindful(ness), 79, 132, 137, 143, 144
morality, 2–3, 8, 9, 12
"morning pages," 156–58, 159, 160
Myers-Briggs Type Indicator (MBTI), 89–91

narcissism, 127, 131

old age, 12, 28, 29, 89, 151
original sin. *See* sin, original
Otto, Rudolph, 59

pain, 22
    benefits of, 27
    holistic, 22–37
panentheism, 46, 68, 69
Paul (apostle), 14, 24, 25, 66, 79, 95, 96, 99, 106
Peck, M. Scott, 4, 72, 95
Penfield, Wilder, 55
Picasso, Pablo, 155, 169
Plato, 17
Plotkin, Bill, 5
prayer, 86

Reeve, Christopher, 82–83
religion, religious, 8, 12, 72, 73, 92
    goal of, 138
retirement, 120

Rogers, Carl, 125
Rohr, Richard, 34

samtusta, 137
samyojana, 135–36
scripture
    as lens, 65
second birth, 12–13, 15, 17
second half of life (phase 2A, 2B), 5, 6, 9, 11–16, 91, 92
Self, 17, 18, 55, 56, 78, 136, 155
    False, 16, 31–33, 98
    True, 16, 31–33, 98
Seligman, Martin, 114
shadow self, 6n3, 49n3, 98
sin
    and healing, 52
    original, 24, 85
    and suffering, 23–24
Skinner, B. F., 125
Smith, Adam, 115
Smith, Huston, 54, 55, 56
snacking, 144–45
Socrates, 8
soul, ix, 16, 19, 31, 32, 33, 54, 55, 56
spirit, 18–19, 50, 54, 55, 56
Spirit. *See* Holy Spirit
spiritual, spirituality, ix, x, 9, 12, 13, 15, 19, 31, 34, 43, 45, 52, 56, 69, 76, 77, 81, 93, 136, 138, 140, 153
    definition of, 56
    and health, 39
    and psychology, 18–20, 75–76
suffering. *See* pain
Sulmasy, David, x

Tao, Taoism, 95
theology
    definition of, 54
    holistic, 54–69
Tiresias, 169
Tolle, Eckhart, 80
Tournier, Paul, 26, 28, 35

Underhill, Evelyn, 16–18, 30
unemployment, 31, 108, 120, 122

Index

Watson, John, 125
wellness, ix, 49, 50, 51, 52
Whitehead, Alfred North, 59, 69
Wizard of Oz, 34
work
    and boredom or lack of challenge, 114–18
    as "calling," 118–20
    and financial compensation, 112–14
    holistic, 108–22
Wright, N. T., 65

Yates, William Butler, 31
yin/yang, 66

www.ingramcontent.com/pod-product-compliance
Lightning Source LLC
Chambersburg PA
CBHW071450150426
43191CB00008B/1298